Gambling

Editor: Danielle Lobban

Volume 420

independence
educational publishers

First published by Independence Educational Publishers

The Studio, High Green

Great Shelford

Cambridge CB22 5EG

England

© Independence 2023

Copyright

This book is sold subject to the condition that it shall not, by way of trade or otherwise, be lent, resold, hired out or otherwise circulated in any form of binding or cover other than that in which it is published without the publisher's prior consent.

Photocopy licence

The material in this book is protected by copyright. However, the purchaser is free to make multiple copies of particular articles for instructional purposes for immediate use within the purchasing institution. Making copies of the entire book is not permitted.

ISBN-13: 978 1 86168 880 4

Printed in Great Britain

Zenith Print Group

Acknowledgements

The publisher is grateful for permission to reproduce the material in this book. While every care has been taken to trace and acknowledge copyright, the publisher tenders its apology for any accidental infringement or where copyright has proved untraceable. The publisher would be pleased to come to a suitable arrangement in any such case with the rightful owner.

The material reproduced in **issues** books is provided as an educational resource only. The views, opinions and information contained within reprinted material in **issues** books do not necessarily represent those of Independence Educational Publishers and its employees.

Images

Cover image courtesy of iStock. All other images courtesy of Freepik, Pixabay and Unsplash, except pages 32 & 34: iStock.

Additional acknowledgements

With thanks to the Independence team: Shelley Baldry, Tracy Biram, Klaudia Sommer and Jackie Staines.

Danielle Lobban

Cambridge, January 2023

Contents

Chapter 1: About Gambling

10 amazing gambling industry statistics in the UK	1
Gambling culture then and now	3
Industry statistics – November 2022	5
Lockdown's impact on gambling	8
Loot boxes, eSports & skins betting	9
Understanding women's experiences of gambling	10
Going for bloke: gambling as a men's health issue	12
Global: a peek into a gambling attitudes	14

Chapter 2: Problem Gambling

Gambling: what happens in the brain when we get hooked – and how to regain control	16
'I blew hundreds of thousands playing online bingo – then I tried to kill myself': the rise of the female gambling addicts	18
Does rugby league have a gambling problem?	22
Gambling in video games is turning kids into addicts – the next PM needs to act	24
David Zendle on video game monetisation	26
Signs of gambling harm	27
Named and shamed: the A-listers – and football clubs – making millions from online gambling's misery	28
How UK gambling safeguards fail to defend online punters	30
Football Index's collapse reveals a deeper rot in UK gambling industry	32
Match-fixing an increasing threat as global sports betting turnover surpasses €1.45 trillion for the first time	34

Chapter 3: Solutions

NHS launches new gambling addiction clinics to meet record demand	35
Gambling needs more holistic management to reduce harm when it causes debt, new research suggests	36
Supporting schools to tackle and prevent gambling harms	38
'Stop promoting them': victims call for football to end tragic link with gambling	39
Five steps to self-care if you gamble	40
Further Reading/Useful Websites	42
Glossary	43
Index	44

Introduction

Gambling is Volume 420 in the issues series.. The aim of the series is to offer current, diverse information about important issues in our world, from a UK perspective.

About Gambling

Recent research has revealed around 44% of UK adults regularly participate in some form of gambling – from buying a lottery ticket to betting on football. The gambling industry is extremely profitable but at what cost to society? This book explores recent trends in gambling, the impact it has when it becomes a problem and the efforts to tackle addiction.

Our sources

Titles in the issues series are designed to function as educational resource books, providing a balanced overview of a specific subject.

The information in our books is comprised of facts, articles and opinions from many different sources, including:

- Newspaper reports and opinion pieces
- Website factsheets
- Magazine and journal articles
- Statistics and surveys
- Government reports
- Literature from special interest groups.

A note on critical evaluation

Because the information reprinted here is from a number of different sources, readers should bear in mind the origin of the text and whether the source is likely to have a particular bias when presenting information (or when conducting their research). It is hoped that, as you read about the many aspects of the issues explored in this book, you will critically evaluate the information presented.

It is important that you decide whether you are being presented with facts or opinions. Does the writer give a biased or unbiased report? If an opinion is being expressed, do you agree with the writer? Is there potential bias to the 'facts' or statistics behind an article?

Activities

Throughout this book, you will find a selection of assignments and activities designed to help you engage with the articles you have been reading and to explore your own opinions. Some tasks will take longer than others and there is a mixture of design, writing and research-based activities that you can complete alone or in a group.

Further research

At the end of each article we have listed its source and a website that you can visit if you would like to conduct your own research. Please remember to critically evaluate any sources that you consult and consider whether the information you are viewing is accurate and unbiased.

Issues Online

The **issues** series of books is complimented by our online resource, issuesonline.co.uk

On the Issues Online website you will find a wealth of information, covering over 70 topics, to support the PSHE and RSE curriculum.

Why Issues Online?

Researching a topic? Issues Online is the best place to start for...

Librarians

Issues Online is an essential tool for librarians: feel confident you are signposting safe, reliable, user-friendly online resources to students and teaching staff alike. We provide multi-user concurrent access, so no waiting around for another student to finish with a resource. Issues Online also provides FREE downloadable posters for your shelf/wall/table displays.

Teachers

Issues Online is an ideal resource for lesson planning, inspiring lively debate in class and setting lessons and homework tasks.

Our accessible, engaging content helps deepen student's knowledge, promotes critical thinking and develops independent learning skills.

Issues Online saves precious preparation time. We wade through the wealth of material on the internet to filter the best quality, most relevant and up-to-date information you need to start exploring a topic.

Our carefully selected, balanced content presents an overview and insight into each topic from a variety of sources and viewpoints.

Students

Issues Online is designed to support your studies in a broad range of topics, particularly social issues relevant to young people today.

Thousands of articles, statistics and infographs instantly available to help you with research and assignments.

With 24/7 access using the powerful Algolia search system, you can find relevant information quickly, easily and safely anytime from your laptop, tablet or smartphone, in class or at home.

Visit issuesonline.co.uk to find out more!

issues online
resources for schools, colleges & libraries

Chapter 1

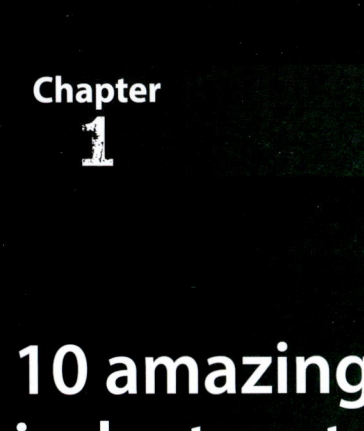

About Gambling

10 amazing gambling industry statistics in the UK

By Mark Baker, UK Tech News Editor

The gambling industry continues to grow worldwide, and remains a major tech employer. One of the main contributing factors comes from online wagers.

A recent report claimed the online gambling market may grow by $142.38 billion between 2021 and 2026. Between 2021 and 2022, the market grew by an estimated 11.82%.

The Gambling Act of 2005 sought to regulate the online gambling industry in the UK The world's top gambling companies have their headquarters in London.

Here's an in-depth perspective of the UK gambling industry.

Most popular form of online gambling in the UK: The National Lottery

The National Lottery remains the most popular form of online betting in the UK. In 2017, 8.6% of survey respondents bet on National Lottery draws.

That number increased to 14% by September 2021. An extra 8% also gambled on another lottery.

At 4.9%, wagers on sports betting stayed the same. Betting on horse races increased from 1.8% to 2.6%.

45-54 year olds gambled online the most between 2020 – 2021

The top age group that gambled online the most in the UK between 2020 – 2021 were 45-54-year-olds. They represented 32.8% of those surveyed.

The rest broke down as follows:

- 35-44 year olds: 28.8%
- 55-64 year olds: 28%
- 25-35 year olds: 25.2%
- 65+ year olds: 18.8%
- 16-24 year olds: 15.8%

An estimated 48% of UK bettors gambled at least once a week in 2021

Almost 34% of bettors in the UK gambled once a month/less than once a week in 2021. Out of the 1,690 respondents, 26.9% said they gambled once a week.

About 21% claimed they bet more than two days per week.

That represented 48.1% of UK bettors who gambled at least once weekly.

Non-remote betting decreased by 57.1% between April 2020 – March 2021

The COVID-19 pandemic increased the popularity of online gambling. That trend continued among UK gamblers between April 2018 and March 2019.

Non-remote betting decreased from a gross gaming yield (GGY) of £3,261 million to £2,416 million between April 2018 – March 2020.

According to the UK Gambling Commission, non-remote GGY dropped again between April 2020 – March 2021 to £1,037 million.

That represented a reduction of 57.1%.

Remote betting increased by 13.5% between April 2020 – March 2021

The UK Gambling Commission also reported an increase in remote betting. Between April 2020 – March 2021, remote betting GGY grew by 13.5%.

That trend represented three years of consecutive growth.

Between April 2018 – March 2019, remote betting generated £2,021 million in GGY. It grew to £2,330 million and £2,645 million in the following two years.

46.1% of remote bettors between April 2020 – March 2021 gambled on football

Two sports also saw three years of consecutive growth among remote bettors. Between April 2020 – March 2021, 46.1% of remote betting GGY came from football.

During that same period, horses took 32.4% of remote betting GGY. (Other categories included betting on dogs, tennis, and cricket.)

Key Facts

- The National Lottery remains the most popular form of online betting in the UK. In September 2021, 14% of survey respondents bet on National Lottery draws.
- The top age group that gambled online the most in the UK between 2020 – 2021 were 45-54-year-olds.
- An estimated 48% of UK bettors gambled at least once a week in 2021.
- Slots represented the most popular online casino game between April 2020 – March 2021.
- The UK gambling industry is one of the top betting markets in the world. The most popular brands include the National Lottery, William Hill, and Bet365.

Discuss

In pairs, discuss what you think are the main reasons for the increase in online or 'remote' gambling in recent years? Write down your thoughts and share with the rest of the class.

GGY of remote bingo increased for five straight years

The Gambling Commission began tracking statistics on remote bingo in April 2015. Since then, GGY has increased for five straight years.

At a rate of 37.1%, its steepest incline occurred between April 2016 – March 2017.

Remote Casinos Grew by 22.5% in the wake of COVID-19

The COVID-19 pandemic brought UK land-based gambling establishments to a halt. Between April 2020 – March 2021, the GGY of non-remote casinos dropped by 88.5%.

Remote casinos benefited from that decline. During the same period, their GGY increased by 22.5%.

Online casinos: UK gamblers bet on slots the most

Slots represented the most popular online casino game between April 2020 – March 2021. Among remote casinos, slots generated 72.5% of GGY.

Roulette came next with 13.2%. Blackjack took in 4.9% of GGY during that period.

Online slots continue to surge in growth. Today, many options exist to play online slots for real money.

Year-on-year gambling among UK adults increased by 43% (March 2022)

Adults in the UK who gambled at least once a month increased by 43% YoY in March 2022. That represented a 3% increase from the previous YoY period.

Online wagers also continue their long-term growth trends. The rise in the availability of casino apps remains a major contributor.

Conclusion

The UK gambling industry is one of the top betting markets in the world. The most popular brands include the National Lottery, William Hill, and Bet365.

These companies stay favoured by men and women, Baby Boomers, and millennials.

With easy access to online apps and a simple internet connection, gambling continues to thrive in the UK.

17 August 2022

The above information is reprinted with kind permission from UK Tech News.
© 2023 UK Tech News

www.uktechnews.co.uk

Gambling culture then and now

By Our Culture Mag & Partners

Throughout recorded human history, and in every corner of the world, gambling has existed in some form or another. It seems that gaming and wagering is as much a part of our collective cultural heritage as music, folklore, or visual arts.

But while gambling has been around as long as humanity, there have been dramatic shifts in how and why we gamble, and in the societal attitudes towards these activities. Even within living memory, there have been profound changes in how gambling is regulated and carried out, and also in how it is presented and perceived.

Gambling has gone from being widely banned to almost universally accepted within less than a century. Today many people think nothing of searching for online casino sign up bonuses, while the parents of those same people may well have viewed gambling as immoral. How is it that gambling culture has changed so much in such a relatively short time?

A troubled past

For centuries, lawmakers have grappled with how to legislate gambling activities. One the one hand, betting and gaming has long been seen as a vice, a sinful pastime condemned by religious leaders. On the other hand, there is money to be made, and state-run lotteries have long been used as a way to fill government coffers. Gambling taxation is mentioned in historical texts that go back as far as the 4th century BC.

Around the middle of the 20th century, there were some more concerted efforts to formalize gambling laws in both the US and the UK. In the US, it was Nevada that first used gambling as a form of economic relief after the Great Depression, leading to the foundation of Las Vegas as the world's most famous gambling destination. However, within a few years the city had become synonymous with organized crime, and the association of gambling with vice became even more firmly entrenched.

In the UK, sports wagering was always the most popular form of gambling, especially horse and greyhound racing. In 1960 a bill was passed legalizing many forms of gambling and allowing licensed betting shops to open for business. Since then, high street bookmakers have been a staple of UK towns and cities across the country.

Changing attitudes

Towards the end of the 20th century, cultural attitudes to gambling remained divided, and often inconsistent. Movies like the James Bond franchise popularized an image of casinos as a suave, elegant, and sophisticated destination. For the rich, at least, a casino was synonymous with glamour.

That image was at odds with the more widespread reality. While many European casinos did embody old-world elegance, for the most part gambling venues were far from glamorous. Bingo halls, racetracks, and betting shops were not for the glitterati. In the US, casinos were often dingy halls filled with slot machines, or garish and brightly lit.

The mob still had a grip on Vegas until the mid 1980s, when the long campaign by the federal authorities finally turned the tide on Mafia involvement with casino gambling. This could be seen as the starting point for a softening in attitudes towards gambling. As the Mafia associations weakened and fell away, what had once been edgy, possibly attractive but certainly licentious, started to become more benign in the collective consciousness.

Modern game-changer

Around the world, and in the US and UK in particular, existing gambling legislation remained more or less fit for purpose until the turn of the century. The late 1990s saw the emergence and the rapid ascendance of online casinos, leading to the next big shift in attitudes towards gambling. While all forms of gambling had slowly become more socially acceptable in the preceding decade, this innovation would prove to be a game-changer.

Where once gambling had been limited by location or social status, online casinos made it accessible to all. Gambling became democratized, an effect that only grew as internet access increased. Early regulators and licensing bodies were non-government, like the Kahnawake Gaming Commission, or based in dubious territories.

It wasn't long before the governments of the world realized that they needed to get some control of the situation. Around the world there have been varying approaches to regulating online gambling, but overall the change has been in the same direction. Cultural opinions about gambling have become far more liberal than at any time in the last century.

The UK in particular leaned into the promotion of gambling culture, passing the 2005 Gambling Act and updating it in 2014. Tax revenue from betting and gambling amounts to around 3 billion British pounds per year. Advertising at sporting events, and on post-watershed television, is dominated by gambling companies from sports betting to bingo.

Where now?

For the time being, it seems that gambling has become almost universally accepted as a form of entertainment, and a taxable source of income for governments worldwide. While some countries have for now decided to forgo formal regulation, the majority of jurisdictions have accepted that internet gambling is here to stay.

Despite some concerns over aspects of online casinos and gambling in general – money laundering, problem gambling, improper practices – the widespread attitudes tend towards acceptance. Already a multi-billion dollar market, the pandemic years saw an even greater number of people turn to online gambling as a leisure activity.

Accurate statistics are hard to come by, but some studies suggest that around a quarter of the global population gamble regularly. This is most certainly a lot more than it was a couple of decades ago. In the US and Canada, individual states and provinces continue to liberalize laws on sports betting and internet gambling. In Europe, each passing year sees more countries establishing their own gambling licensing and regulatory bodies.

There will always be those who view gambling as a vice to be avoided, but the cultural shift has resulted in that being a minority opinion. In 2020, a Gallup poll found that a record percentage of Americans – 71% – viewed gambling as a morally acceptable activity. Not so long ago, such a statistic would have been inconceivable.

21 February 2022

Key Facts

- Gambling has gone from being widely banned to almost universally accepted within less than a century.
- Gambling taxation is mentioned in historical texts that go back as far as the 4th century BC.
- In the US, it was Nevada that first used gambling as a form of economic relief after the Great Depression, leading to the foundation of Las Vegas as the world's most famous gambling destination.
- In the UK in 1960 a bill was passed legalizing many forms of gambling and allowing licensed betting shops to open for business.
- The UK passed the Gambling Act in 2005 and updated it in 2014. Tax revenue from betting and gambling amounts to around 3 billion British pounds per year.
- In 2020, a Gallup poll found that a record percentage of Americans – 71% – viewed gambling as a morally acceptable activity.

Think...

Consider the following questions and write your answers down.

- What is a bookmaker?
- Where is the world's most famous gambling destination?
- When was the UK Gambling Act passed?

The above information is reprinted with kind permission from ourculture.
© 2023 Our Culture Mag Limited

www.ourculturemag.com

Industry statistics

Summary

Gambling Industry Statistics report on the size and shape of the customer-facing gambling industry in Great Britain.

This report provides an overview of Gross Gambling Yield (GGY) made by licensed gambling operators from Great British (GB) gambling customers for each customer-facing sector, along with the numbers of licensed operators and premises. It is based on data reported to us by the operators we license and regulate. The accompanying data file includes figures for all sectors, based on data from April 2021 to March 2022, as well as historical data back to 2009.

Various lockdown rules and restrictions throughout the last two reporting periods have significantly impacted the gambling industry. These measures were most severe during the reporting period April 2020 to March 2021, though at the beginning of the latest period considered in these statistics, lockdown restrictions were still in the process of being lifted.

We have not included estimated figures where returns have either been late or are not yet due, as we would not expect the previous period's heavily pandemic affected figures to be comparable to the figures from this reporting period. We accept that this may result in some figures which underestimate the actual totals. The methodology used for estimations in previous publications is available on our website.

Details

Remote gambling

Remote Casino, Betting and Bingo (RCBB) accrued £6.4 billion Gross Gambling Yield (GGY) which can be broken down into 3 individual areas:

- online casino games dominate the sector, generating £3.9 billion in GGY, £3.0 billion of which was from slots games
- GGY for remote betting totalled £2.4 billion, led by football (£1.1 billion) and horse betting (£768.5 million)
- GGY for remote bingo totalled £183.5 million.

This reporting period saw a decrease in the number of new account registrations with RCBB operators (down 1.0 percent to 32.6 million). In comparison to the latest pre-lockdown period however, there is an increase by 9.1 percent. The number of active accounts went up 7.0 percent to 31.9 million and 5.9 percent from pre-lockdown. The total funds held in customer accounts was at £910.5 million at the end of the reporting period. This is a £16.7 million (1.9 percent) increase on the previous period end and a £217.9 million (31.5 percent) increase on the last pre-lockdown period end.

Key Facts

- £14.1 billion - Total Gross Gambling Yield (GGY) of the Great Britain gambling industry (April 2021 to March 2022) (10.9% (percent) increase from April 2020 to March 2021 and 0.8% decrease from April 2019 to March 2020)
- £9.9 billion - Total GGY of the gambling industry in Great Britain (excluding all reported lotteries) (April 2021 to March 2022) (16.5% increase from April 2020 to March 2021 and 2.4% decrease from April 2019 to March 2020)
- 8,408 - Total number of premises in Great Britain (31st March 2022) (2.5% decrease from 31st March 2021 and 17.1% decrease from 31st March 2020)
- 6,219 - Total number of betting shops in Great Britain (31st March 2022) (3.8% decrease from 31st March 2021 and 19.1% decrease from 31st March 2020)
- £6.4 billion - Total GGY for Remote Betting, Bingo and Casino Sector (April 2021 to March 2022) (6.2% decrease from April 2020 to March 2021 and 12.4% increase from April 2019 to March 2020)
- £3.5 billion - Total GGY for Land-based Sectors (Arcades, Betting, Bingo and Casino) (April 2021 to March 2022) (110.5% increase from April 2020 to March 2021 and 21.5% decrease from April 2019 to March 2020)
- £1.8 billion - Total GGY for gaming machines in Great Britain (April 2021 to March 2022) (96.3% increase from April 2020 to March 2021 and 12.6% decrease from April 2019 to March 2020)
- £1.7 billion - Primary Contributions (to good causes) from The National Lottery (April 2021 to March 2022) (0.5% decrease from April 2020 to March 2021 and 3.4% increase from April 2019 to March 2020)
- £417.0 million - Contributions to good causes from large society lotteries (April 2021 to March 2022) (3.8% increase from April 2020 to March 2021 and 13.4% increase from April 2019 to March 2020)
- 2,419 - Gambling operators in the market (31 March 2022) (0.9% decrease from March 2021 and 6.3% decrease from March 2020)
- 3,339 - Gambling activities licensed (31 March 2022) (0.9% decrease from March 2021 and 5.5% decrease from March 2020).

Non-remote gambling

Non-remote betting Gross Gambling Yield (GGY) was the third largest sector by GGY with £2.1 billion (a 105.6 percent increase on the previous lockdown heavy period and a 11.9 percent decrease on the latest pre-lockdown period).

GGY at venues (on-course), at betting shops (off-course), and pool betting all replicated the increase and decrease with reference to lockdown and pre-lockdown periods. Within off-course data, machines GGY increased by £590.6 million to £1.0 billion during the last period but decreased

Gambling industry GGY (£m)

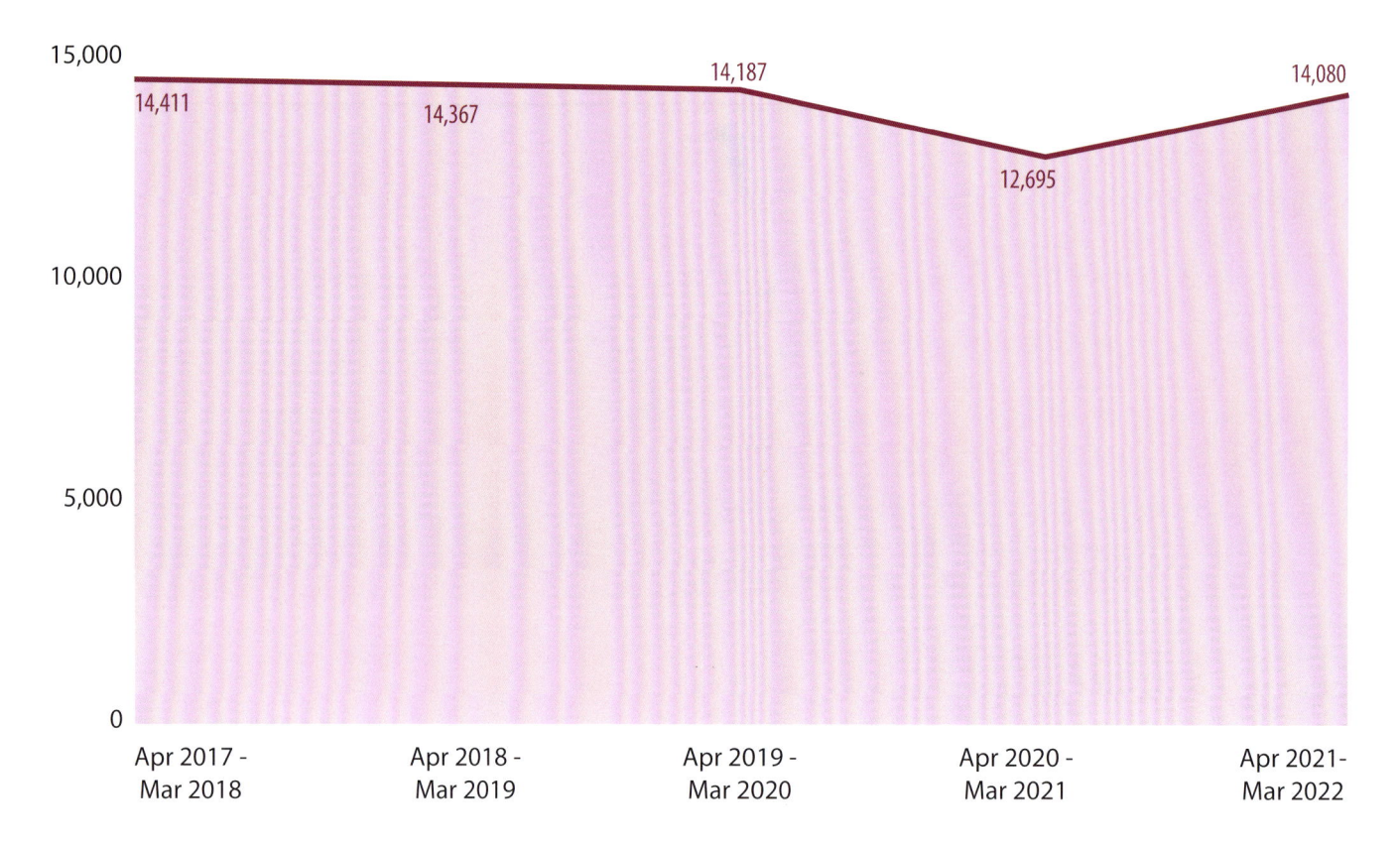

Period	GGY (£m)
Apr 2017 - Mar 2018	14,411
Apr 2018 - Mar 2019	14,367
Apr 2019 - Mar 2020	14,187
Apr 2020 - Mar 2021	12,695
Apr 2021 - Mar 2022	14,080

by £13.6 million (1.3 percent) from the latest pre-lockdown period. Machines represented 50.0 percent of total GGY in the non-remote betting sector.

Total numbers of betting premises have continued to decline for the eighth consecutive reporting period to 6,219 (19.1 percent down on the pre-lockdown period).

The non-remote casino sector saw a £575.1 million increase in GGY to £691.8 million (casino games at £511.2 million and casino machines at £180.6 million) for this last reporting period. This followed a decrease of £900.9 million in GGY (casino games by £718.1 million and casino machines by £182.8 million) during the lockdown heavy period.

Non-remote bingo GGY saw a £142.5 million increase to £388.6 million (bingo games at £147.4 million and bingo machines at £241.2 million) for this last reporting period. This followed a decrease of £330.1 million (bingo games by

£14,080 Million
Industry GGY

10.9%
Change from previous period

Gambling industry GGY by sector for latest period

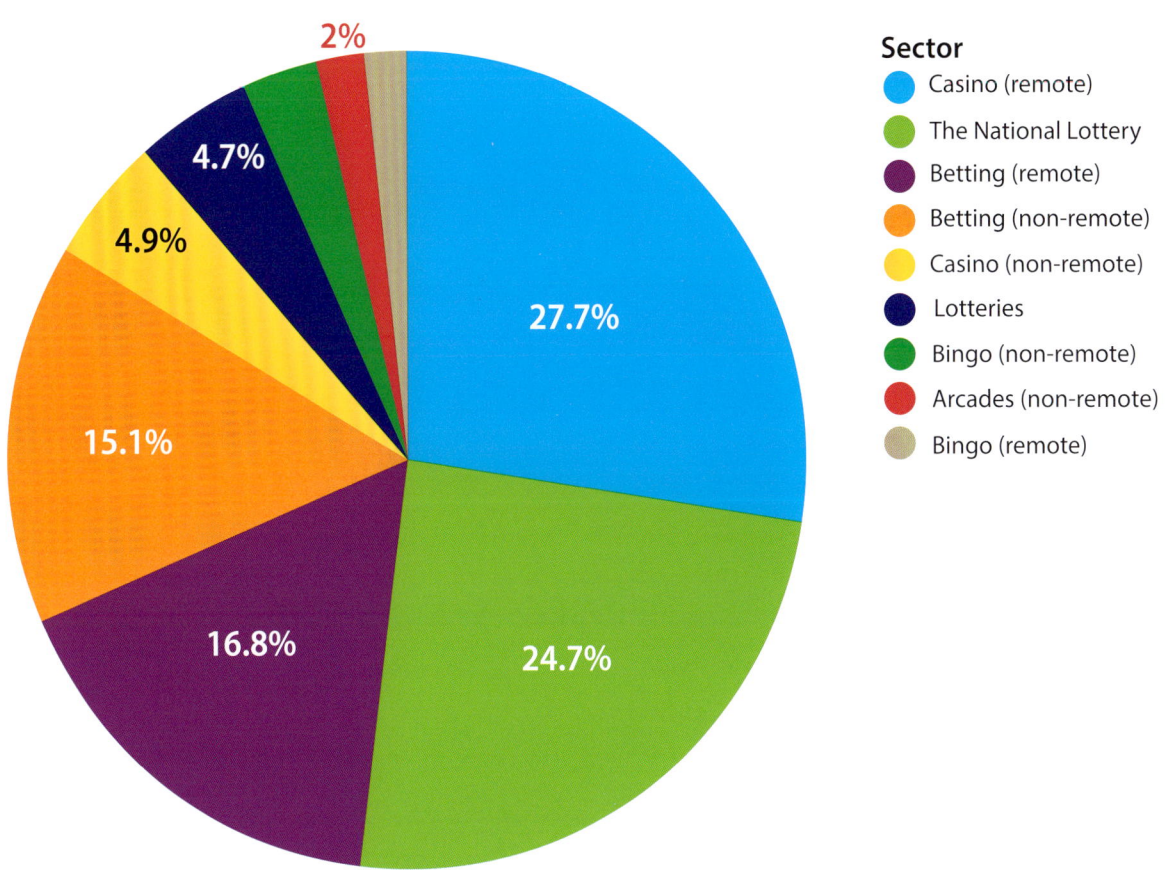

Sector	%
Casino (remote)	27.7%
The National Lottery	24.7%
Betting (remote)	16.8%
Betting (non-remote)	15.1%
Casino (non-remote)	4.9%
Lotteries	4.7%
Bingo (non-remote)	2%
Arcades (non-remote)	
Bingo (remote)	

Key Points:
Overall industry GGY increased by £1,385.3m (10.9%) from £12,694.9m to £14,080.2m between periods April 2020 - March 2021 and April 2021 - March 2022. Increases by sector were seen in betting (non-remote) by £1,092.6m (105.6%), casino (non-remote) by £575.1m (492.8%), bingo (non-remote) by £142.5m (57.9%), Lotteries (remote and non- remote) by £30.7m (4.8%) and arcades (non-remote) by £20.2m (7.8%). Between the same periods GGY decreased in betting (remote) by £280.9m (-10.6%), casino (remote) by £141.0m (-3.5%), National Lottery (non-remote and remote) by £48.4m (-1.4%) and bingo (remote) by £5.5m (-2.9%). Between periods April 2017 - March 2018 and April 2021 - March 2022 industry GGY decreased by £330.4m (-2.3%) from £14,410.6m to £14,080.2m.

Notes:
For The National Lottery and lotteries, figures are a GGY equivalent. For lotteries, this includes any GGY equivalent raised through external lottery managers. Sales from operators with gaming machine technical, trading rooms only and gambling software licensed activities are not included in these charts.

Source: The Gambling Commission

£170.1 million and bingo machines by £160.0 million) during the lockdown heavy period.

In the arcades sector, adult gaming centres showed a GGY increase of £21.7 million (9.3 percent), to £255.4 million for this last reporting period. This followed a decrease of £149.1 million during the heavy lockdown period. GGY for licensed family entertainment centres decreased, by 5.9 percent to £22.9 million. This followed a decrease of £23.8 million during the heavy lockdown period. Note that this data does not include family entertainment centres which operate using a permit from a local authority.

Lotteries

During April 2021 to March 2022 The National Lottery ticket sales totalled £8.1 billion, of which £4.6 billion was returned as prizes and the primary contribution to good causes totalled £1.7 billion. Each of these were lower than the previous period (by 3.5 percent, 5.0 percent and 0.5 percent respectively) however, they were higher than in the April 2019 to March 2020 reporting period (by 2.4 percent, 2.4 percent and 3.4 percent respectively).

During April 2021 to March 2022 lotteries (excluding The National Lottery and small society lotteries) ticket sales totalled £919.1 million, of which £253.3 million was returned as prizes and the contribution to good causes totalled £417.1 million. Each of these are the highest figures reported to date, comprising increases of 5.4 percent, 7.0 percent and 3.8 percent, respectively, compared to 2020-21 and increases of 10.4 percent, 15.5 percent and 13.4 percent, respectively, compared to 2019-20.

24 November 2022

The above information is reprinted with kind permission from Gambling Commission.
© Crown Copyright 2023
This information is licensed under the Open Government Licence v3.0
To view this licence, visit http://www.nationalarchives.gov.uk/doc/open-government-licence/

www.gamblingcommission.gov.uk

Lockdown's impact on gambling

One third of regular sports betters stopped betting completely during the UK's first lockdown.

A new report studied the gambling behaviours of regular betters before and after the first UK lockdown from March to June 2020.

The work was led by researchers at the universities of Glasgow and Stirling, and funded by the Economic and Social Research Council.

A marked decrease in gambling

Dr Heather Wardle from the University of Glasgow said:

'Unsurprisingly, our study found that, during the initial lockdown in March 2020, with the closure of gambling venues such as bookmakers, and a huge reduction in live sports, there was a marked decrease in sports gambling.'

The study found that 17.3% of men and 16.5% of women started a new form of gambling during the same period.

Additionally, 31.3% of men and 30.3% of women increased their frequency of gambling on at least one activity. The study found those who started a new form, or increased the frequency of gambling during lockdown, are potentially vulnerable to gambling harms.

Dr Wardle said:

'These findings are important and suggest that regulators and the industry should be looking closely at how behaviours are changing during national lockdowns, and doing more to protect people from harms.'

New types of gambling activity

Professor Kate Hunt from the University of Stirling said:

'Our study found that, among regular sports bettors, restrictions in supply during lockdown generated changes in behaviour, including reductions in gambling for the majority, who did not appear to seek out other ways to gamble.

However, when examining online sports betting, a minority continued to bet as some horse races and sports were still available in other countries. Furthermore, some people also started gambling on new types of activity – including the lottery and virtual online sports – that they had not previously engaged in.'

The findings, published in the journal *Addictive Behaviours*, will help inform the review of the Gambling Act 2005, currently being conducted by the Department for Digital, Culture, Media, and Sport.

17 June 2022

The 'Lockdown's impact on gambling' article was published by the Economic and Social Research Council (ESRC) about research it funded as part of UK Research and Innovation's (UKRI) rapid response to Covid19 (grant number ES/V004549/1). The full research report and acknowledgements are available here: https://www.sciencedirect.com/science/article/pii/S0306460321000617

Create

In pairs, create an infographic to illustrate the key statistics in this article.

The above information is reprinted with kind permission from UK Research and Innovation.
© 2023 UKRI

www.ukri.org

Loot boxes, eSports & skins betting

Loot boxes

- Typically, a loot box is an in-game mechanic which will reward you with a random prize.
- Within some games, you will have the chance to use credits you have earned or purchased using real world money.
- Loot boxes come in many different forms (boxes, crates, packs of cards, spinning wheels, slot machines).
- When opened, loot boxes often have sounds and graphics that raise excitement levels and anticipation.

eSports

- eSports is a form of competition that takes place electronically, most often in the form of video games. Some eSports professionals make money from gaming competitively online and in packed out arenas
- eSports is a popular spectator sport, with an estimated global audience of up to 150 million people. As such it has become an attractive betting proposition.
- Popular eSports Games include *Defense of the Ancients* (DOTA), *League of Legends* (LOL), *Counter Strike Global Offensive* (CS:GO) and *Overwatch*.

Skins betting

Skins are mostly cosmetic items players can purchase in a variety of games for players to customise their characters. Players can buy, sell and exchange these items. When these items are used as virtual currency to bet on the outcome of professional matches or other games of chance, that is defined as skins betting.

Time consumption

Some players may spend a lot of time on a social game. This is especially common on games that have an immersive world, or customisable characters. The physical implications (inactivity, repetitive strain injury, sleep deprivation) go hand in hand with social implications, such as social isolation, or lack of self-care.

In-game purchasing

In-app or in-game purchasing can be a very easy way to run up a significant bill. With one tap, players can buy bonuses, level ups, hints etc., and quickly lose control of spending limits.

Key issues with eSports

eSports and betting have become more closely linked in recent times, however eSports is popular with a young demographic and many fans are under the legal age to gamble.

Though proportionally there is little gambling on e-sports taking place in the mainstream market, there are more opportunities to place bets in unregulated markets. This is a of particular concern in relation to young people.

eSports matches are also streamed for free on the web, via sites like twitch.tv, which can also include promotion for different forms of gambling.

The Gambling Commission has started to consider this as an issue of concern, along with skins betting. etc.

2022

The above information is reprinted with kind permission from Big Deal
© 2023 Big Deal

www.bigdeal.org.uk

issues: Gambling　　　　　　　　　　Chapter 1: About Gambling

Understanding women's experiences of gambling

Today marks International Women's Day 2022, providing a moment to share what we know about women and gambling.

Historically, the gambling experiences of women have been somewhat hidden amongst nationally representative statistics and high-level trends. It's easy to revert to long-held assumptions about preferred activities and less frequent participation, but when we dive deeper we can get a much better understanding of what motivates women to gamble, how they engage with different products, and how gambling fits into their day to day lives.

Here, we use some of our core telephone survey data and qualitative consumer research, along with other recent studies, to explore how women gamble and the impact that their own or someone else's gambling can have on them.

How do women engage with gambling?

Our latest participation data shows that nearly half (42%) of women have gambled in the last four weeks, predominantly on activities such as the National Lottery draws, other lotteries, scratchcards and bingo. Women aged 35-54 are most likely to gamble (32%), with slightly lower participation amongst younger and older age groups. Lotteries and scratchcards are universally popular, but younger women are also gambling privately with their friends, and playing fruit and slot machines in gaming centres and arcades.

'I don't gamble very much – just a bit of fun now and then. I'll go to casino, bingo or the dogs maybe once a year. The odd arcade in summer.' – Female gambler, aged 39.

We also know that online gambling is becoming increasingly popular amongst women of all ages (having increased by 8 percentage points between 2017 and 2021), particularly those aged over the age of 35. This is being driven in part by women switching from playing National Lottery draws in person, to playing them online. However, women are also beginning to engage in online gaming products.

Data analysed by NatCen and the University of Liverpool suggests that women who have online gambling accounts (for online slots, casino, bingo and instant win products), actually tend to play more often, for longer, and spend more than men.

'I often play online bingo at home in my lounge or my bedroom if the hubby is watching football. I use either my tablet or phone. If I haven't won with my £10 limit then I will come off the game for a couple of days. I play around two to three times a week.' – Female gambler, aged 22.

What motivates women to gamble?

We know that online gambling products such as slots and casino games are often enjoyed by people who want to have some 'me time' and relax – whether it be in a break at work, or at the end of the day – however, there are lots of different reasons why people gamble. For many women, gambling provides an opportunity to be sociable and enjoy time with friends, with activities such as gambling at casinos, going to the bingo and playing machines in arcades providing the opportunity to gamble whilst having fun with others.

'Me and my best friend have a little routine since we were 18, we always go to the casino together. We start off doing our own thing on our favourite machines and then we pool our winnings and go on the roulette table.' – Female gambler, aged 32.

issues: Gambling — Chapter 1: About Gambling

However, gambling carries some risk and for many that is never too far from consideration.

'I have a love hate relationship with gambling. I have seen it cause a lot of problems, but I can see the benefit of it for entertainment. I feel everyone should be allowed to do it, but vulnerable people should be more protected.' – Female gambler, aged 26.

What do we know about gambling harms experienced by women?

Our latest prevalence data suggests that the problem gambling rate (using the mini-screen PGSI) is 0.2% amongst women, with the moderate and low risk rates at 0.9% and 1.4% respectively. The problem gambling and low risk rates are both lower than male counterparts, however in 2021 we have seen the moderate risk rate 'balance out', and the rates for men and women have become almost equal. We will be exploring the data further to understand why this might be.

It's important to note here that there have, for a while, been questions about the suitability of the tools that are being used to accurately measure and identify female problem gamblers and some have suggested that the statements covered by the PGSI may not be as effective for women as they are for men. This is a really important area that we're working to better understand.

One way we are trying to unpick this issue is by improving our understanding of the broader harms that are caused by gambling, which will allow us to zoom in on what these experiences are like for women. From our early piloting of this work, we know that female gamblers are particularly likely to have experienced harms to their mental health, wellbeing and finances. A further dimension is the fact that women are also more likely to be experiencing harm as a result of someone else's gambling rather than their own, with their relationships and financial security being affected.

These harms can often be hidden, and yet have serious and long-term impacts. Treatment and support is another area where an understanding of women's own experiences is vital. GambleAware are currently exploring this in research conducted by IFF Research, the University of Bristol and GamCare's Women's Programme, the first phase of which recommended approaches to enable women to access support for gambling harms. GambleAware has also launched its first ever harms prevention campaign specifically aimed at women to help them to identify critical warning signs and seek support before gambling becomes harmful.

Key Facts

- Online gambling is becoming increasingly popular amongst women of all ages (having increased by 8 percentage points between 2017 and 2021), particularly those aged over the age of 35.

- Data analysed by NatCen and the University of Liverpool suggests that women who have online gambling accounts (for online slots, casino, bingo and instant win products), actually tend to play more often, for longer, and spend more than men.

- Women are more likely to experience harm as a result of someone else's gambling rather than their own, with their relationships and financial security being affected.

Moving forward

As an evidence-based regulator it is essential that the data we collect gives us the most accurate picture available of gambling behaviour. As we strive to improve the quality of our statistics, we are currently piloting a new survey methodology which will improve the robustness and timeliness of our participation and prevalence data.

If successful, we hope the survey will be rolled out on a continuous basis with a much larger sample size than our existing quarterly telephone survey. This will significantly enhance our ability to understand gambling behaviours amongst subgroups of the population, including women, and to enable us to better tell the stories of their experiences and identify ways that we can improve regulation and reduce gambling harm.

8 March 2022

Research

Conduct a survey among your female classmates, friends or family and find out the following information:

- Have they ever placed a bet or taken part in any gambling activity?
- If 'yes', what type of gambling activity did they pursue?
- How many gamble online?

Write a short report of your findings and illustrate them with a graph or a pie chart.

The above information is reprinted with kind permission from Gambling Commission.
© Crown Copyright 2023
This information is licensed under the Open Government Licence v3.0
To view this licence, visit http://www.nationalarchives.gov.uk/doc/open-government-licence/

OGL

www.gamblingcommission.gov.uk

Going for bloke: gambling as a men's health issue

Peter Baker, Director, Global Action on Men's Health, explains the gender split in gambling and how this can be addressed.

By Peter Baker

Gambling, especially problem gambling, is more common in men than women. 45% of men and 40% of women gambled in some way in 2020, according to Gambling Commission data.

There is a much bigger sex gap when it comes to problem gambling – 0.6% of men are defined as 'problem' gamblers (those 'who experience negative consequences and a possible loss of control') compared to a statistically insignificant proportion of women. Twice as many men as women (1.3% vs 0.6%) are 'moderate risk' gamblers (those who 'experience a moderate level of problems leading to some negative consequences').

Over three quarters (78%) of active online betting accounts are held by men and the online betting sector derives an estimated 94% of its revenue from men; among the highest spending accounts (where £5,000 or more was spent over the year), over 95% were held by men, typically in their 40s. 70% of callers to the National Gambling Helpline are male.

Much of the explanation lies in male socialisation. Men often feel the need to demonstrate their masculinity through acts that are sensation-seeking and risk-taking. Gambling, especially high stakes gambling, may provide men with the opportunity to show how skilled and fearless they can be, traits often considered desirable in men. Men who engage in 'strategic' forms of gambling – such as casino table games – have been found to display higher levels of conformity to masculine norms.

More than women, men are attracted to gambling because of impulsiveness, the excitement of the activity, the chance to win rewards, and the search for immediate satisfaction. Men can get drawn into more serious addiction by a need to escape negative emotions generated by the game (e.g. money loss, debt, conflict, lies to family members and close people). The behaviour is therefore maintained by a pattern of negative reinforcement.

Male problem gamblers are significantly more likely than females to boast about winning to others and to swear at or be rude towards staff in gambling venues. Female problem gamblers, on the other hand, are much more likely to cry. Men are more frequently angry, more likely to hit gaming machines, and to play aggressively. Male problem gamblers are also more likely to groan aloud or blame the venue or machine when they lose, and to drink while gambling. Men can also act territorially and try to scare away other customers from gaming machines they have 'claimed' for themselves.

The greater prevalence of gambling problems in men does not of course mean that women's gambling problems should be overlooked. Gambling is certainly not just a men's health issue. In fact, there is good evidence that women's gambling has been under-researched, become more common in recent years, and causes more problems than is generally recognised.

Higher levels of mental distress and more suicidal behaviour has been reported in female problem gamblers than male. Women can also be significantly affected by men's problem gambling, not least when it impacts on family income and causes relationship difficulties. What matters more than which sex has a higher proportion of problem gamblers is whether sex and gender are taken into account in understanding why problem gambling occurs and how it should be addressed. The benefits of a 'gendered' approach are now increasingly well-recognised in other areas of public health.

Tighter controls on gambling – such as stake caps, affordability checks, bans on gambling advertising and sponsorship, and an end to VIP schemes – would no doubt help to limit both male and female participation. Prohibiting gambling advertising in sport, particularly football, could be particularly helpful for men – it has been suggested that gambling logos are on screen for 70% of the time during *Match of the Day*. Including gambling in the health education curriculum in schools should also make a difference.

Greater investment in mental health interventions targeted at men would be beneficial as would increasing men's awareness of the impact of traditional notions of masculinity on health behaviours and of the benefits of adopting different ways of being male. The major changes in men's role as fathers over the past 50 years suggest that 'traditional' masculinity is by no means unmalleable.

Destigmatising male help-seeking for problem gambling could be helped by the use of case-studies of other men who have benefitted from support services, harnessing the voices of male role models, providing support that is anonymised and confidential, and locating face-to-face services in 'male-friendly' venues (such as sports stadia, providing of course they are gambling-free zones).

The current Gambling Act review must take a gender-responsive approach to ensure that both men and women are protected from unnecessary harm. The Department of Health and Social Care recently announced that it will consult on a women's health strategy for England. This is much-needed, and so too is a complementary strategy for men that addresses all aspects of their unnecessarily poor health outcomes, including as a result of problem gambling.

23 March 2021

Key Facts

- Gambling, especially problem gambling, is more common in men than women.
- Over three quarters (78%) of active online betting accounts are held by men and the online betting sector derives an estimated 94% of its revenue from men.
- 70% of callers to the National Gambling Helpline are male.

Debate

'It has been suggested that gambling logos are on screen for 70% of the time during *Match of the Day*.' Do you think gambling advertising should be banned? Split the class into two groups: one group will argue in favour of a ban and the other will argue against it.

The above information is reprinted with kind permission from Royal Society for Public Health

Baker P. blog [Internet]. London: RSPH. Going for bloke: Gambling as a men's health issue. March 2021. Available at https://www.rsph.org.uk/about-us/news/going-for-bloke-gambling-as-a-men-s-health-issue.html#:~:text=Men%20often%20feel%20the%20need,often%20considered%20desirable%20in%20men Accessed on 3 November 2022.

© RSPH 2023

www.rsph.org.uk

Global: a peek into gambling attitudes

As industry players chase international growth, our new tool – YouGov Global Gambling Profiles – sheds light on the biggest gambling markets around the world, as well as the differences in gambler behaviour and attitudes. YouGov Global Gambling Profiles continuously collects data in 24 countries to allow users unique, real-time insights into how much the world gambles and why.

Gambling for enjoyment: where is betting enjoyed most?

YouGov Global Gambling Profiles data provides marketers with insights into people's attitudes towards gambling right around the world. Today, we can reveal which countries enjoy betting the most.

Global: where is gambling most enjoyed?

% of adults who agree with the statement 'I really enjoy betting'

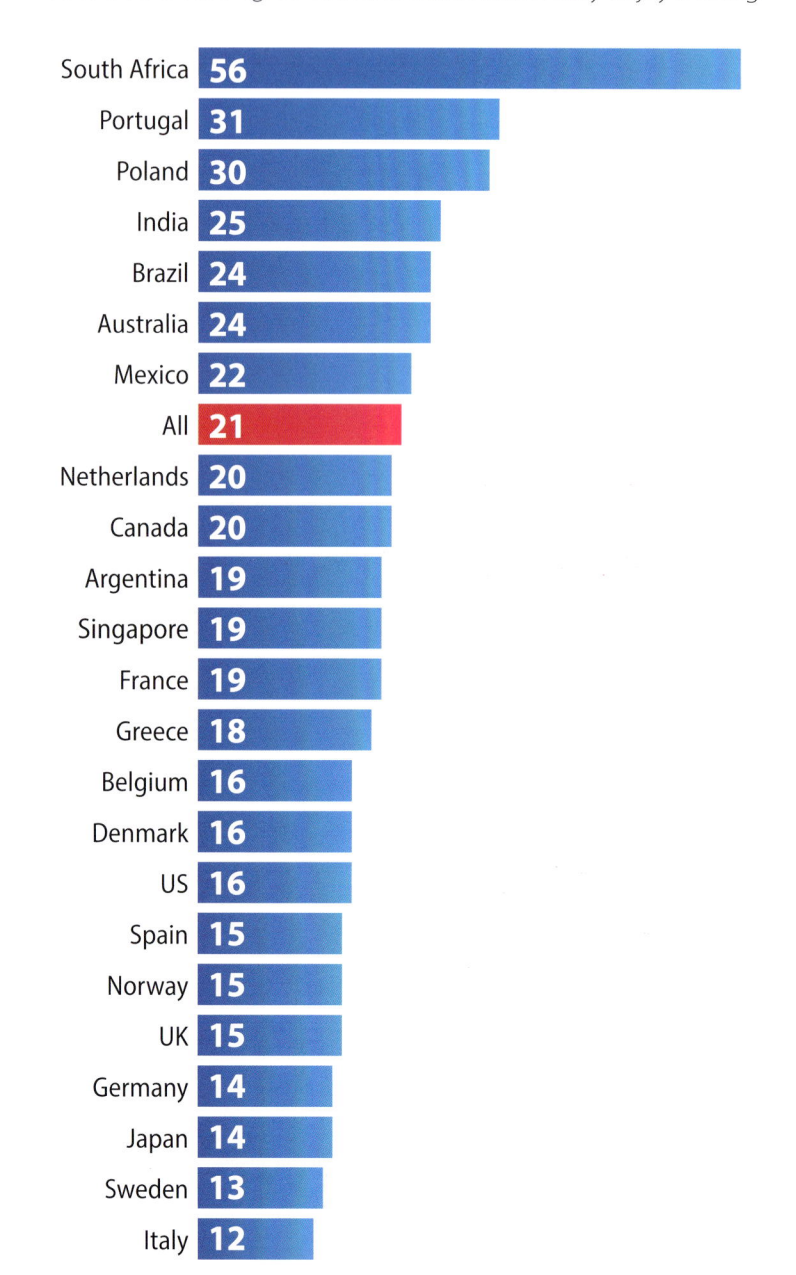

Country	%
South Africa	56
Portugal	31
Poland	30
India	25
Brazil	24
Australia	24
Mexico	22
All	21
Netherlands	20
Canada	20
Argentina	19
Singapore	19
France	19
Greece	18
Belgium	16
Denmark	16
US	16
Spain	15
Norway	15
UK	15
Germany	14
Japan	14
Sweden	13
Italy	12

Our data reveals that more than one in two (56%) adults in South Africa say they 'really enjoy betting', compared with just 21% globally.

Poland (30%), Portugal (31%), Brazil (24%) and India (25%) are some of the other markets where a significant proportion of adults say they really enjoy betting.

Fantasy sports is popular across the world

The tool also gives us an insight in the modes of gambling that are the most popular in each market. Sports betting as a broad category is a favourite in almost all markets. But the preferences for different sub-categories of sports-based gambling are highly varied. Let's take a closer look at the popularity of fantasy sports and esports betting in each market.

There seems to be a much higher appetite for these new formats of gambling in emerging markets like Brazil, India, Mexico and South Africa. In Brazil, where 39% of consumers say they would place more bets if it was easier to do so, a high share of consumers express interest in esports (30%) and fantasy sports (27%) betting as well. The opposite is true in more-established gambling markets such as the UK and Denmark, where far fewer people also appear to be impeded by a lack of ease in placing bets.

Fantasy sports – a more interactive form of sports gambling – has gained increasing visibility in some markets in recent years. We take a broader look at this relatively novel form of sports betting.

South Africa seems to be the biggest untapped market for fantasy sports, especially when you combine this data with the insight that 57% of South Africans say they would bet more if it were easier to do so. Again, developing markets like India show a high interest in fantasy sports generally, while more mature markets like the US, Australia and the UK all fall around the global average

Consumer preferences: knowing what's important to gamblers

So when people have decided to gamble, what informs their bet?

Data from Global Gambling Profiles reveals that a large share of gamblers – two-fifths of them – cite fun and enjoyment as an important factor when placing bets. Three in ten gamblers (30%) cite favourable odds as a factor they consider important when placing a bet, while over a quarter (27%) of them are driven by hunches.

Pertinently for marketers, one in five (20%) of those who place money on bets say that available promotions are an important factor when they think of gambling.

issues: Gambling   14   Chapter 1: About Gambling

Interest in gambling on fantasy sports and esports tends to be much higher in emerging markets

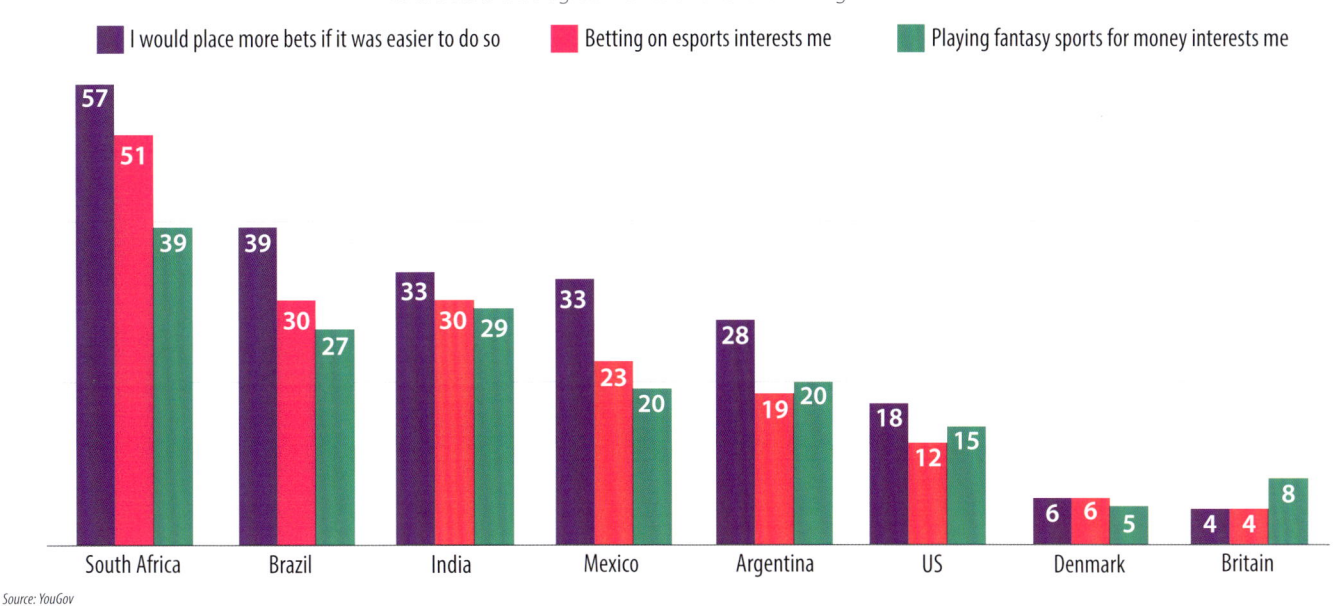

% of adults who agree with each of the following statements

- ■ I would place more bets if it was easier to do so
- ■ Betting on esports interests me
- ■ Playing fantasy sports for money interests me

Country	More bets if easier	Esports betting	Fantasy sports
South Africa	57	51	39
Brazil	39	30	27
India	33	30	29
Mexico	33	23	20
Argentina	28	19	20
US	18	12	15
Denmark	6	6	5
Britain	4	4	8

Source: YouGov

Global: appetite for gambling on fantasy sports

% of adults who agree with the statement 'playing fantasy sports for money is something that interests me'

Country	%
South Africa	39
India	29
Brazil	27
Argentina	20
Mexico	20
Singapore	18
Portugal	15
US	15
Poland	14
All	14
Australia	12
Italy	12
Canada	12
Spain	12
Greece	11
UK	8
Netherlands	8
Norway	8
Belgium	7
France	7
Japan	7
Germany	6
Sweden	5
Denmark	5

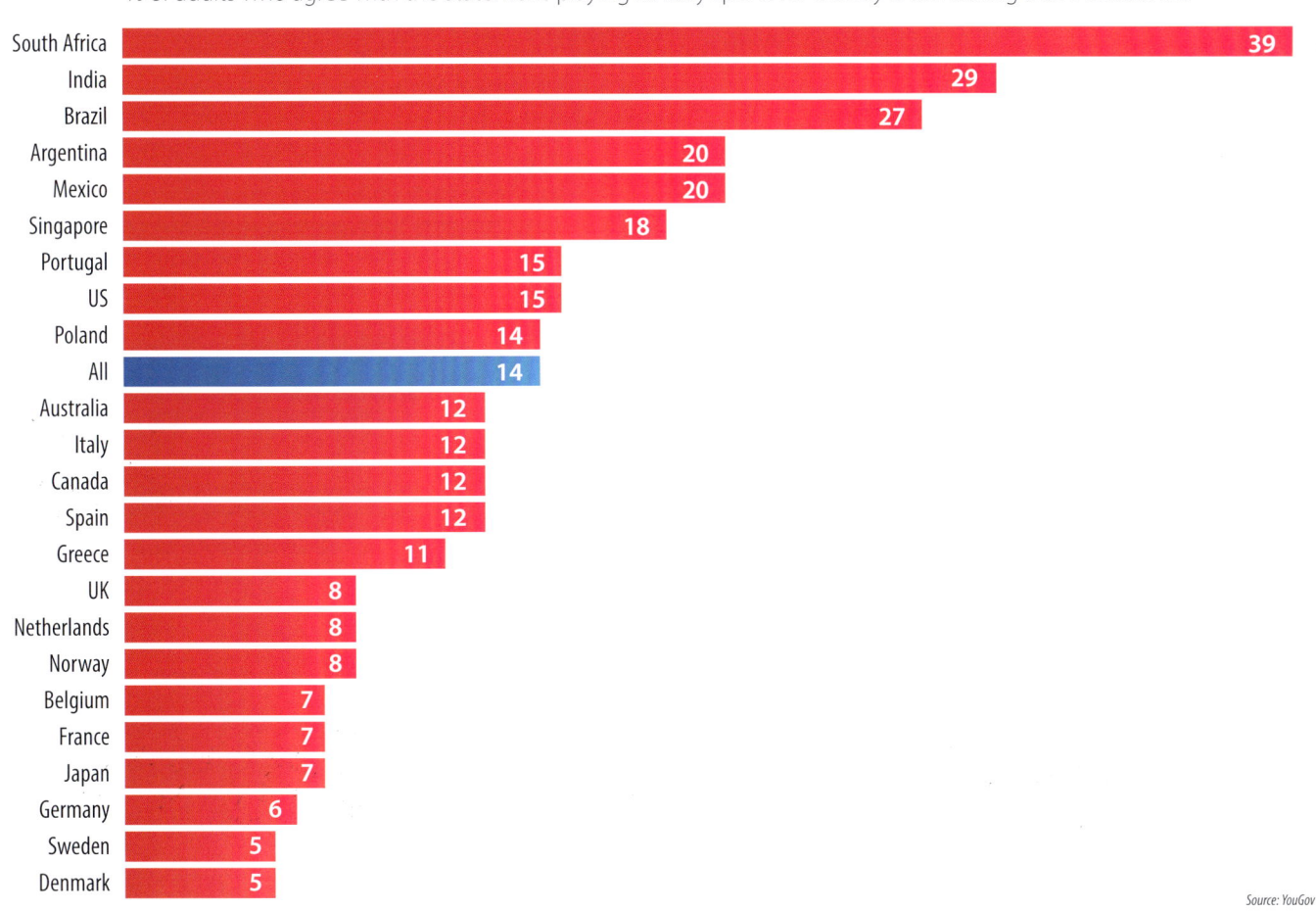

Source: YouGov

Methodology: YouGov Global Gambling Profiles, which includes data from 24 countries, is based on continuously collected data from several sources, rather than from a single limited questionnaire. Data referenced is based on a sample size of between 1,661 to 2,102 adults. Online interviews were conducted in April 2021.

7 July 2021

The above information is reprinted with kind permission from YouGov.
© 2023 YouGov PLC

www.yougov.co.uk

Problem Gambling

Chapter 2

Gambling: what happens in the brain when we get hooked – and how to regain control

An article from The Conversation.

By Barbara Jacquelyn Sahakian, University of Cambridge, Christelle Langley, University of Cambridge, Henrietta Bowden-Jones, University of Cambridge and Sam Chamberlain, University of Southampton

Many people turned to online gambling during the pandemic. And while a large proportion of us are able to gamble recreationally, without serious negative impact, the pandemic has led to a rise in gambling addictions. In the UK, for example, we've seen the biggest increase in women seeking help ever. Such addiction can lead to problems with mental health, cognition and relationships, as well as leading to bankruptcy and criminality.

Unlike alcohol and drug addiction, where the symptoms are physically noticeable, gambling addiction creates less obvious signs. Our new article, published in *The Lancet Psychiatry*, reviews research on gambling addiction, and makes recommendations about how to best prevent and treat it.

Gambling is a huge problem. According to the most recent estimate from the World Health Organization, from 2016, players' annual global gambling losses were estimated to total US$400 billion (£295 billion). In 2021, the UK's Gambling Commission estimated that prevalence of 'gambling disorder' was 0.4% of the population.

Another survey found that the highest rates of problem gambling were in Asia, followed by Australasia and North America, with lower rates in Europe.

Researchers have developed game simulations (which they call 'tasks') to measure problem gambling, such as the Iowa Gambling Task and the CANTAB Cambridge Gambling Task. In the latter, which assesses risky decision-making and betting, participants are asked to guess whether a yellow chip is hidden within a blue or red box, with the ratios of blue and red boxes changing over time. They can then decide how many of their points to bet on their decision.

If they win, they add the points to their total, but if they lose, those points are lost. They are told to be careful not to go 'bankrupt' – losing all their points. This task may be able to detect those gamblers who are 'at risk' of developing a gambling disorder, but may not be there yet – particularly if they show signs of being impulsive.

Using such tasks, research has shown that betting, in healthy individuals, is most common in people between the ages of 17 and 27 and declines as we get older. Another study showed that gamblers with addiction problems tend to increase their betting over time, and end up going bankrupt. Alcohol and nicotine dependency have also been linked to greater betting problems

The gambler's brain

From neuroimaging studies, it is clear that there are several brain regions associated with gambling. Studies have shown that important regions associated with risky decision-making include the ventromedial prefrontal cortex (involved in decision-making, memory and emotion regulation); orbital frontal cortex (which helps the body respond to emotions); and insula (which regulates the autonomic nervous system). Problem gamblers may therefore have increased activity in these areas.

When gamblers watch the results of their bet, they also show increased brain activation in the reward system of the brain, including the caudate nucleus. This may be particularly strong in people who are addicted to gambling.

Dopamine, a so-called neurotransmitter which helps nerve cells to communicate, is also known to be an important chemical in the brain's reward system. One study also found that problem gamblers showed significantly higher levels of excitement when dopamine was released in their brains compared to healthy people. Dopamine release seems to reinforce problem gambling through increasing excitement levels, reducing inhibition of risky decisions, or a combination of both.

In addition, the nucleus accumbens, which plays a role in processing reward, has been shown to be involved in risky behaviours in adolescents and adults. This region is rich in dopamine and suggests a further role for dopamine in risky behaviours.

Tackling gambling addiction

Currently, gambling disorder is diagnosed using the Diagnostic and Statistical Manual of Mental Disorders (DSM-5) published by the American Psychiatric Association. Guidelines for the treatment and management of gambling disorder from the National Institute for Health and Care Excellence in the UK are also being developed and expected to be published in 2024.

Current treatment options include certain forms of cognitive behavioural therapy (which can help people change their thinking patterns) and self-help groups. Some medications, such as selective serotonin reuptake inhibitors (SSRIs) may be effective in reducing aspects of gambling disorder symptoms, such as depression.

We also know that opioid receptors in the brain help it process rewards, and have long been suspected to be drivers of addiction. We discovered that there is some evidence indicating that a drug called Naltrexone, which blocks opioid receptors, may help some people with gambling disorder. But more research is required before this can become a standard treatment.

There are also things you can do yourself to control your gambling. The NHS Live Well website provides information for services available for problem gamblers. It offers tips such as paying your bills before you gamble, spending time with friends and family who do not gamble, and dealing with your debts. Gamblers would also be wise to avoid seeing gambling as a way to make money, stop bottling up their worries about gambling habits and avoid taking out credit cards to pay for gambling.

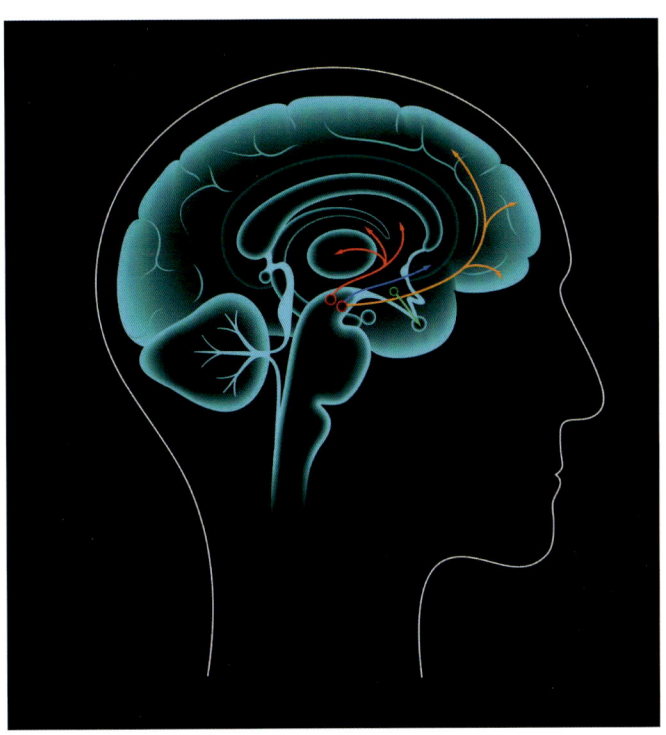

As with all mental health problems, the key is to get early support and treatment. This is especially important so that normal rewards, such as spending time with family and enjoying walks and exercise, are still pleasurable and the reward system does not get hijacked by gambling.

16 February 2022

Key Facts

- Gambling is a huge problem. According to the most recent estimate from the World Health Organization, from 2016, players' annual global gambling losses were estimated to total US$400 billion (£295 billion).

- Another survey found that the highest rates of problem gambling were in Asia, followed by Australasia and North America, with lower rates in Europe.

- From neuroimaging studies, it is clear that there are several brain regions associated with gambling.

- Guidelines for the treatment and management of gambling disorder from the National Institute for Health and Care Excellence in the UK are being developed and expected to be published in 2024.

THE CONVERSATION

The above information is reprinted with kind permission from The Conversation.
© 2010-2023, The Conversation Trust (UK) Limited

www.theconversation.com

'I blew hundreds of thousands playing online bingo – then I tried to kill myself': the rise of the female gambling addicts

By Siobhan Smith, Freelance writer, editor and TV producer

Pottering around her kitchen one night with her laptop open on the table, Bev noticed an advert pop up on her screen.

At that point, she had never gambled before. But the advert was colourful, shiny, and it looked like a bit of harmless fun, and so, without giving it much thought, she decided to deposit a ten pound bet.

Bev, who lives in Newcastle-upon-Tyne, didn't win anything that first time. But she decided to have another go. And then another. Very quickly, she won £800 and couldn't believe her luck.

'I'd never won anything in my life,' she tells Metro.co.uk. 'But it seemed so easy and, so, I decided to keep playing.'

However, what she didn't realise that night was her 'lucky streak' would lead to a ten year gambling addiction and nearly cost her everything – including her life.

Bev is one of a huge number of women who are classed as 'problem gamblers' – and it's a figure that's growing.

'The gambling landscape has significantly shifted and evolved in the past decade or so, mostly due to the rise of accessibility and availability of online gambling,' Zoe Osmond, chief executive of GambleAware, told Metro.co.uk.

'The number of women gambling online has risen by over 50% over the past four years,' she continues. This is almost double the growth rate of men over the same period of time.

'And with the latest data showing that up to one million women may be at risk of experiencing some sort of harm as a result of gambling – be it financial, emotional, or in terms of impacting their relationships with loved ones and leading to isolation – it's critical we drive awareness around early warning signs, such as losing track of time, spending too much, or a tendency to hide gambling from others.'

Despite her initial big money prize, very quickly, Bev lost the £800 and found herself trying to win it back. And then again. And again, as she lost more and more money.

Soon, she found herself placing more and more bets, until she was playing constantly, spending every spare minute – and penny – gambling online.

'I had a good job and I was making around £2,200 after tax – sometimes more. But at the end of every month, I would find myself sitting up until midnight on payday, so I'd see my wages go in. I'd blow the whole lot that night.'

The NHS employee estimates that she's gambled hundreds of thousands in total over the years. 'I had a hundred grand in credit card debt alone, never mind all the loans from friends and family,' she says.

Bev is married with a daughter. At home, she was spending all her time on the computer, but they had no idea what she was doing. She describes making sure she always had her screen facing away from her family, often finding herself sitting in the same room as them, betting hundreds of pounds at a time, with them none the wiser.

Eventually, she ran out of sources for money – she, and by default her husband, were up to their eyes in debt. Bev was in charge of the bills; they weren't getting paid and things got to the point where she had to ask for help.

Initially, nobody could believe it. But, with the help of her husband and sister, the family made a plan to pay back the money that was owed. Everyone – including Bev – thought that would be it. Now that she'd come clean, surely she would stop. But it wasn't as easy as that.

However, despite trying several times to give up, the sites kept enticing Bev back in.

She was depositing so much money – hundreds at a time – that she became known as a 'VIP'. This meant that, when she hadn't played for a few days, she would start getting emails offering her free money to get extra plays – sometimes to the value of hundreds of pounds.

'Then you can't say no to that,' she says. 'It's an awful, predatory tactic.'

This is a huge part of the problem, she says, these sites do their utmost to lure new users in, and to keep bringing old ones back. Often, at great financial cost.

Not long after opening up to her family, Bev found herself taking out more secret payday loans, and defaulting on bill payments again. However, the impact wasn't all financial – as it rarely is.

Gambling in secret took a massive toll on her mental health, her physical health, and her relationships. Her marriage started to suffer, with her husband 'on the edge of a nervous breakdown'.

Then, on Christmas day 2016, it all came to a head. Bev decided to put a bet on. 'My logic at the time was, "surely they won't let you lose at Christmas?"' she says.

'Within 45 minutes I emptied my husband's account and blew £5,000.

'I then took an overdose. That night was when I realised I couldn't carry on like this anymore. I just didn't want to be alive anymore.'

The increase in female gamblers has been on the rise for some time and is likely a result of a few different factors, explains Osmond.

'Since the pandemic, for example, we have seen the rate of growth in online gambling almost triple (36% between 2019-2021, compared to 13% between 2017-2019), with some turning to gambling apps whilst feeling isolated and anxious.'

We also know part of the problem is likely driven by the accessibility of it; it's on our laptops and our phones, therefore within touching distance at all times. And it's easy to hide a screen.

Many women are drawn to online gambling, such as bingo or casino games, as the games are often perceived as more innocent and familiar. They appear very similar to the seemingly innocuous digital games we're used to playing on our phones and, in a similar way, become a form of escapism.

Tracy Galvin, who lives in Essex, says that her addiction made her feel like she was two different people. 'The Tracy who was gambling and the Tracy who was trying to cover it up. It was like having a split personality,' she explains.

Introduced to gambling at the age of 17, Tracy would play the slot machines, after finishing a shift in the bingo hall she worked in.

'It started small,' the mum-of-one remembers. 'And it just got worse and worse.'

Tracy, 58, experienced her first big win one night after she finished work, when she won £250 – a moment she recalls as a turning point.

From there, things escalated and the slot machines quickly became something that she would turn to for escape and comfort. She describes gambling, and the distraction that it created, to fill a void in her life and as a way of dealing with difficult things she had going on.

But it became so much more than that. 'It was on my mind constantly and it got to the point I felt like an outsider looking in on my life,' she says. 'I was a shell of myself.'

Tracy found herself guilty of all three of these. For decades, she spent every spare minute on the slots and was unable to confide in anyone about the extent of her addiction. Emotionally, this was incredibly difficult.

'I've had two nervous breakdowns as I just wasn't able to cope with it all,' she tells Metro.co.uk. 'And financially, I have lived a life of robbing Peter to pay Paul.'

Tracy was working three jobs in order to fund her habit, leaving the house at 7am and getting home at 1am. In between, all she could think about was gambling.

'At the age of 40, I had seven strokes, and spent a year in hospital. I fully believe that this was caused by the emotional damage it was doing.'

'Physically it nearly killed me,' she says. 'I was lucky not to lose my life, but I lost the most important thing: Time.'

After reaching breaking point, Tracy finally went to her first support group. She found that she was the only woman, out of over 50 attendees.

For her, this is part of the problem: female gamblers feel more shame than men and are often more reluctant to ask for help. 'Women are seen to be the nurturer, the homemaker,' she says. 'We have to be the strong ones.'

Since then, Tracy has worked on her recovery, with the help of organisations including Gordon Moody – a charity dedicated to providing support and treatment for gambling addiction.

She successfully obtained a degree in social sciences and recently qualified as an addiction counsellor, as well as supporting others during peer support meetings.

Despite this, Tracy still speaks carefully and with emotion about her addiction, stressing that just because you've stopped, you're not an 'ex-gambler'. It's something that stays with you forever, she says.

According to GambleAware, part of the problem is that women are exposed to a higher number of gambling adverts than men, like Bev was.

A recent report discovered that much of this promotion is found to be especially targeted at women, tending to portray gambling as innocent social fun – and for lotteries, as 'a national pastime', 'for people like us', or about supporting communities.

Bev says she finally sought help after her sister scoured the internet for advice and came across a charity that specialised in supporting those with gambling addictions. It's now been three years since Bev placed her last bet.

She believes that there needs to be more regulation and a duty of care within the industry.

'If affordability checks had been carried out – like they are if you're getting a loan – 99% of problem gamblers probably wouldn't be allowed to play,' she suggests. 'But I was just allowed to continue to deposit and deposit and deposit.'

'To anyone struggling, I want to say that there is help out there. I am living proof.' But, with huge stigmas and shame attached to gambling, it can be hard to ask for help.

It's often dubbed the 'hidden addiction', with recent GambleAware data showing that more than half (59%) of people stated they felt society is judgemental towards those who struggle to stay in control of their gambling.

And this can be even worse for women with almost two in five (38%) people agreeing that society is more critical of women's gambling.

But it's important to remember that there is not a stereotypical 'problem gambler' – it affects people of all ages, from all walks of life.

Liz Karter, MBE is a gambling addiction counsellor and psychotherapist with over 22 years' experience supporting women. She has also published three books on the topic of gambling, addiction and women.

Over the last two decades, Liz has seen it all – and not only has she noticed the rise in female gamblers, she's seen diversification in her clients.

'I run women's groups which are pro-bono as well as a private practice and I would say that 50% of the women I treat are from a more typically middle class, affluent background,' she says.

These are women with high-flying jobs, and people who – from the outside – look as though they've got it all.

'It's not true that people who are less knowledgeable about how to manage money are more susceptible. Lots of the women I treat are from financial backgrounds. I also see doctors, accountants, lawyers. Mainly, it's driven by escapism.'

These women, she says, are the unheard voices – and they are even more reluctant to come forward for help. But there are many.

Liz stresses that she's seen people lose everything. 'I've seen women lose their homes, their marriages, their life's savings – and in some really sad cases I've seen women lose their children,' she says. 'You name a figure, I've seen it.'

But it's not just about trying to win money, explains Liz. Gambling addictions are often a result of people trying to fill a void, or distract themselves from other problems.

'It's very much tied to the stress that women are under these days, trying to do it all,' she says. 'Women with too much responsibility and not enough support.

'Gambling can be meditative,' she continues. 'You're in that world so, temporarily, it puts to sleep other anxious thoughts.

'However, after a while any excitement over initial wins subsides as they get deeper into it, before they find themselves in a pit of despair.'

Jemima*, aged 35, started gambling after becoming a young mum.

Her ex-husband was an alcoholic, drinking every day. Jemima felt that it wasn't safe to leave her son in his care, and was therefore unable to leave the house.

However, feeling ashamed of her situation, she didn't ever confide in anyone. She was lonely and one night online, she decided to try bingo.

For Jemima, it was a form of escapism – and it also became a replacement for the social life that she was sorely missing.

'At the beginning it was fun,' she admits. 'You had a chat forum where you could talk to other people who were playing. It was like a network of friends, and it felt like an alternative to a night out.'

However, struggling to cope with the loneliness and difficulties of her life, Jemima soon found herself gambling constantly and obsessively.

'I got to the point where I was then logging on at night, and before I knew it, I'd hear birds singing outside – and realise that I'd been playing all night.'

What started out as £10 or £20 bets gradually became deposits of up to £600 at a time. In the end, she estimates that she gambled well over £100,000.

'It didn't even feel like real money, it just felt like a number on a screen,' she admits.

Jemima says her life had deteriorated before her eyes.

'Every day I was digging a deeper and deeper hole,' she remembers. 'I could have been in a room with 100 people and I would have felt so alone – because I couldn't tell anyone how I was feeling or what I had going on. I was dead inside.

'That's when I turned to crime to fund that gambling habit.'

Desperate for more money to feed her addiction, Jemima committed fraud, illegally accessing and spending money from a friend's bank account. Realising what had happened, her friend then reported the fraudulent activity to the police.

When Jemima found this out, she turned herself in. She knew she'd go to jail for what she'd done, yet it felt like a relief – as it meant that everything would be out in the open – and it would force her to stop.

After ten months on bail, which Jemima used to try and sort out some of her debt and make sure her son would be ok, she served a total of nine months in custody, and four months on a tag.

Upon her release, she got help from charity Bet Know More UK, who she says were pivotal in getting her life back on track. After volunteering with them, she was offered a job and now uses her experience to help others.

She agrees that the stigma is much worse for women, making it harder to ask for help.

'I think gambling is seen as more typically "male", she says. 'We often think of betting shops and casinos. And, in the glamorous casino scenario we think of the woman being there on the arm, rather than being the ones gambling.'

'I didn't feel able to turn to anyone and admit the mess I'd got myself into – I felt so ashamed.'

Research from GambleAware has found that women's experience of gambling differs from men.

'Stigma, such as feeling ashamed or embarrassed, in particular play a huge role, both in women recognising that they may be experiencing harm, but also in feeling secure and empowered to seek help without being judged,' explains Osmond.

The charity has also found that women experience gambling very differently to men, all the way from their initial motivation through to how they experience harms and how they might seek treatment.

'We also know that women are more likely than men to say their gambling has caused them mental health issues such as stress and anxiety,' adds Osmond.

Following their gambling addiction, Tracy, Bev and Jemima have all received help, and all have turned their lives around, coming back from rock bottom.

They each wanted to stress that help is out there for people who are struggling, or who think they might have a problem.

'Don't be embarrassed or ashamed, you are not alone,' says Jemima.

'We need to break that stigma. It doesn't make you less of a mum, sister, daughter, or person – you're still you.

'The more women that come forward, the more we normalise asking for help. I want people to know that you can get your life back, like I did.'

20 March 2022

* Name has been changed

Design

Design a leaflet to raise awareness of problem gambling. You should include the signs and symptoms of a gambling problem and add sources of help and advice.

The above information is reprinted with kind permission from *Metro*.
© 2023 Associated Newspapers Ltd

www.metro.co.uk

Does rugby league have a gambling problem?

As Betfred takes control of rugby league sponsorship, has the sport backed the right horse?

By Antony Broxton

It was Easter 2004, and two of Britain's top rugby league players stumbled upon one of the best betting opportunities of all time. Ahead of the top-of-the-table clash between Super League giants Bradford and St Helens, Sean Long and Martin Gleeson discovered that one of the sides would be fielding their reserve team. With the bookmakers anticipating a close game, the pair placed large bets on St Helens to lose by 9 points or more. In what the BBC described as a 'a one-sided and hugely disappointing match', Bradford won 54-8 and the pair picked up over £2000 in winnings.

There was, however, just one problem. Long and Gleeson were St Helens players and had placed the bet on their own side to lose. Within days of collecting the cash, the *Daily Mail* investigative team discovered the story and plastered it all over the back pages. Long was doorstepped at his home in Wigan, giving a publicity-shy sport its most notorious headlines in a generation.

The betting 'scandal' triggered a debate within the sport about players' links to the betting industry. As a result, rules on squad announcements were changed, and the RFL opened a hotline for players to anonymously disclose information about the scale of the problem. The following year, clubs 'shied away from a potentially controversial title sponsorship with an online poker business' to prevent any further damage to their brand. By 2012, clubs still wanted to pursue a more 'ethical' sponsorship policy. The game famously turned down a multi-million-pound offer from Betfair in favour of a 'cashless' deal with the haulage firm Stobart. In a sport short on money at the best of times, it turned out to be a financial disaster.

'The Blair Government wanted to unshackle the gambling industry'

In the decade since the Stobart deal, rugby league has radically altered its stance on gambling sponsorship. As the game has sought different structural ways of turning its fortunes around, bookmakers have been its financial saviour. It began with the arrival of Ladbrokes and Coral but has accelerated through the Warrington-based firm Betfred. Faced with declining broadcast revenues, Fred Done – the self-styled 'bonus king' – has stepped in to fund the game. And their domination of the rugby league landscape is absolute. The Betfred Super League sits on top of Betfred Championship and Betfred League One, with the Betfred Challenge Cup as the premier knockout competition. More widely, Betfred is the title sponsor of the growing Women's Super League and the Betfred Wheelchair Super League.

The influence of one sponsor over an entire sport means that however fans choose to watch – whether it is men or women, professional or amateur, in Cornwall or in London, Wigan, Leeds or Newcastle – they constantly come into contact with Betfred advertising.

Whether it is on the side hoardings, pitch markings, corner flags or across the various TV brandings, Betfred is across it all.

Whilst Betfred's sponsorship of the domestic competition has grown, the international game has historically been able to develop different types of sponsors due to its higher profile. That tradition changed last week when Betfred was unveiled as the main shirt sponsor of the England national side for the home World Cup this Autumn. With the tournament able to reach audiences well beyond club supporters, Betfred will be the first sponsor millions of people see when they turn on their televisions in the hope of an England triumph.

Rugby league's decision to fully embrace betting advertising comes at a crucial moment for the future of the industry. The government recently launched a review of gambling laws amid mounting concern over addiction and children's exposure through advertising in sports products. The aim is to reassess Labour's controversial Gambling Act of 2005, which radically altered how betting companies marketed themselves.

Back then, the Blair Government wanted to unshackle the gambling industry from outdated legislation which still restricted the number of shops, casinos and fruit machines in each region. Seeing it as an opportunity to flex free-market credentials, Tessa Jowell, the Minister responsible for bringing in the changes, claimed that opponents of her reforms were 'snobs' who simply found casinos to be 'gaudy and in poor taste'. But because much of the media and parliamentary scrutiny was focused on the new 'super casinos', the changes to bookmaking went by almost unnoticed.

Previously bookmakers had to prove sufficient demand to develop a new shop on the high street. But, as the *Guardian* warned at the time, Jowell's legislation meant that 'there is now little to stop bookies opening up as many shops as they believe the market can take'. Jowell would later acknowledge that the changes had 'blighted London streets'. But for the treasury, it has proved to be extremely lucrative. The industry is now worth over £14bn, with a tax intake amounting to around 0.6 per cent of central government revenues.

One of the biggest changes emerging from the Act was the freedom for firms to advertise and enhance in-play betting. The boom, spearheaded by adverts featuring celebrity endorsements from José Mourinho and Ray Winstone, has helped push betting into the mainstream. But as one RMN mental health nurse has been documenting on Twitter, stories of the impact of addiction are never far from the media.

For Tom Fleming, the Communications Manager at Gambling with Lives – which is leading a campaign to change the legislation – sports are a way for firms to 'normalise gambling and make gambling companies household names by exposing fans and young people to them'. But while much attention is placed on the impact on our national game, rugby league has not even begun to have a debate about the effect.

Rugby league administrators are keen to argue that Betfred's positive influence goes well beyond their financial support. RFL Chief Executive Ralph Rimmer posed with Betfred owner Fred Done at the launch of the new England jersey last week. He told the media that Betfred is the 'perfect partner' for a home World Cup that he believes will be the most 'diverse' ever seen. But the challenge Rimmer faces is the one that the leaders of the game have always faced: how to square creating a different image for the sport with the need to bring in hard cash.

In the 1970s and 80s, the sponsors who aligned themselves with rugby league fitted its image as the sport of the industrial manual worker. Cigarette brands such as State Express, JPS, Embassy and Silk Cut pumped millions into the game. Northern breweries such as Whitbread, Stones, John Smith's and Tetley's aligned their brands to the game while British Coal embodied the link with coal communities across the North. Yet while the game needed to move beyond those sponsors eventually, the sport has never been in a position where one sponsor has dominated every division and every cup it can sell.

One of the main aims of the switch in the summer of 1996 was to diversify its corporate sponsors and bring new supporters on board. National brands such as JJB Sports, Kellogg's and Powergen all bought into the changes, while the national side attracted the support of British Gas, Gillette and Guinness. When, in 2004, the finance company Engage came on board, it was seen as a significant symbol of change: 'It is no surprise,' argued the RFL Chief Executive Richard Lewis, 'that is a financial services company.' It reflected how the sport had 'moved and is positioning itself very deliberately and professionally'.

'Bookmakers predominantly grip the sponsorship of the game'

Rugby league supporters should question how the sport ended up putting the entire house on Betfred, just as other sports are moving in the opposite direction. Crystal Palace recently became the first Premier League club to remove a gambling sponsor with clubs expected to agree to a voluntary ban on shirt sponsorship soon. The FA has already cut ties, while those who continue to pursue deals, such as Sunderland in the Championship, have faced backlash from supporter groups. Legislation is changing in Spain and Holland, while in Australia, where the problem is arguably worse, two NRL teams have committed to 'challenge the idea that betting is a normal part of sport' through the Reclaim the Game programme.

Rugby League is not yet ready to be part of the discussion about what happens next. England head coach Shaun Wane – the man tasked with selling the team to the nation this year – was frank when he admitted that without Betfred, 'we would struggle' as a sport. Wane believes the sport is so indebted to Betfred that he has promised to dedicate a World Cup win to Fred Done: 'Hopefully, if we can do something this World Cup, it will be for Fred,' he recently said. Others have gone further. The owner of Leigh Centurions recently argued that French supporters offer less to the game because they 'can't use Betfred'.

Nobody doubts Betfred's millions have helped sustain the sport through the pandemic. Whilst it is inevitable that rugby league would partner with a bookmaker for some sponsorship, there is a trade off when it is so dominant. Jon Dutton, the organiser of the World Cup, recently announced that there will be 'many similarities with the women's Euros' this autumn with games having a 'festival' atmosphere and 'celebration'. In many ways, rugby league does generate a similar atmosphere at its major events with more women, young children and families in attendance than at other sports. But as one person who attended the Euros' final this week pointed out, one of the most refreshing aspects of the game was the absence of gambling sponsorship in the ground.

Rugby league's success this autumn rests upon whether it can bring in new audiences to the sport who would not normally watch a domestic game. Part of that means connecting the players with the country and developing an image of the game within the wider sporting consciousness. Rugby league, like the Lionesses, is not blessed with ready-made celebrities and mega stars. But it does have down-to-earth players rooted in their communities. When the COVID-19 crisis hit, players were at the forefront of the organisational response in their towns, from coordinating welfare checks and running foodbanks to raising money for NHS services. This is a game with values that other corporate sponsors should be eager to align themselves with.

For now, it is the bookmakers that predominantly grip the sponsorship of the game. Recently, the pollster Survation found that a third of football supporters would not buy their team's shirt if it had a gambling logo on it. England fullback Sam Tomkins believes that if England wins the World Cup, 'every kid' will want to buy the replica jersey. But the restrictions in place on advertising to children mean that they will not be able to buy the same branded shirt as their heroes.

In October, when the World Cup kicks off in Newcastle, betting adverts featuring celebrities and sports stars likely to appeal to children will be banned by the Committee for Advertising Practice. The tide is clearly beginning to turn away from Labour's liberal gambling reforms. As rugby league continues headfirst in the opposite direction, supporters may wonder whether the sport has backed the right horse.

7 August 2022

The above information is reprinted with kind permission from *The Critic*.
© 2023 Locomotive 6960 Limited

www.thecritic.co.uk

Gambling in video games is turning kids into addicts – the next PM needs to act

The government has washed their hands of the duty of regulating what is effectively gambling in a form of entertainment played by children.

By Max Anderson

For too long, we have ignored the fact that gambling mechanics – spending money for an uncertain reward – have infested some of our favourite childhood pastimes. Whoever the new prime minister will be, if they want to meaningfully address the issue of problem gambling in this country, they must tackle the spread of gambling mechanics in digital space.

Arguably, when we look back to our childhood, we can find these mechanics everywhere: opening a Kinder Surprise egg, collecting 'Match Attax' or 'Panini' football stickers, or battling with Pokémon cards. For years, we spent our pocket money buying these things in the hope of receiving that rare or special reward that would help us win that next game, or make us the envy of the playground.

Although they might seem harmless in this form, technological development has given these mechanics a far more menacing and accessible shape. Playground card games have been replaced by their virtual equivalents through 'loot boxes' – digital boxes that reward players with random items in exchange for money or in-game currency. We see this in online games such as FIFA, a football emulator that has over 9 million unique players every year.

At best, these forms of gambling mechanics offer a cruel and exploitative outlet for addicts; at worst, they act as a 'gateway' to future gambling addictions.

This trend is even more alarming in the context of the UK's gambling epidemic. YouGov estimates the UK has up to 1.4 million problem gamblers – people whose gambling addiction has become harmful to themselves or others. The Gambling Commission suspects 50,000 of these are children.

For many, this gambling addiction doesn't take place inside casinos and betting terminals, but in their living rooms. Teenager Jonathan Peniket talked about spending his university loan and family savings on FIFA loot boxes, addicted to the gambling mechanics within the game. But these mechanics don't just target adults. There are numerous stories of children spending as much as £6,000 on FIFA loot boxes.

When these gambling mechanics are combined with a feeling among children and adults of being 'pressured' to buy the loot boxes to remain competitive with their friends – as without the best cards you won't remain competitive – we get a dangerous mixture of addiction and peer pressure.

How have we got this far without anything being done? The main reason is due to the legal definition of gambling. As the Gambling Commission has stated, gambling is when, 'via a game of chance', money, or something that can be exchanged for a monetary value, is received, and they argue that loot boxes fall outside of this.

It is up to the government to set clearer boundaries, but despite the similarities between gambling in games and more recognisable forms of gambling, ministers have been slow to evolve with technology. They have failed to recognise the significant value and advantage that each loot box reward can provide – and the negative effects that can result. Furthermore, a number of video game companies, such as Valve, have allowed players to trade items for money or an equivalent, therefore attaching a monetary value to the reward.

Meanwhile, the Department for Digital, Culture, Media and Sports – despite acknowledging the harm of loot boxes and similar developments – have instead called upon gaming companies to reform and regulate themselves, rather than take any concrete action. Effectively, the government has washed their hands of the duty of regulating what is effectively gambling in a form of entertainment played by children and adults alike.

Without necessary government-imposed reform, companies will be left to self-regulate whilst facing no consequences for failing their duty of care. In fact, they are more likely to have an incentive to continue deploying gambling-like mechanics, as games like FIFA make four times the amount of money from 'live services' like loot boxes than from actually selling the game.

This presents an opportunity for the incoming prime minister to set a new trend when it comes to gambling in the digital space and prove that the UK government will no longer continue to be on the back foot when it comes to digital policy. The new prime minister should take the initiative and take action on loot boxes, helping to tackle the UK's problem gambling problem.

18 August 2022

Max Anderson is senior communications officer at Bright Blue, a pressure group for liberal conservatism, and has written extensively on digital policy and mental health.

Key Facts

- YouGov estimates the UK has up to 1.4 million problem gamblers.
- The Gambling Commission suspects that 50,000 of the UK's problem gamblers are children.

The above information is reprinted with kind permission from *The Independent*.
© independent.co.uk 2023

www.independent.co.uk

David Zendle on video game monetisation

Dr David Zendle is a leading researcher into the links between gaming and gambling. In this guest blog, he explains how games have become sales platforms – and how policy changes, including a gaming regulator, could help safeguard play.

By Dr David Zendle

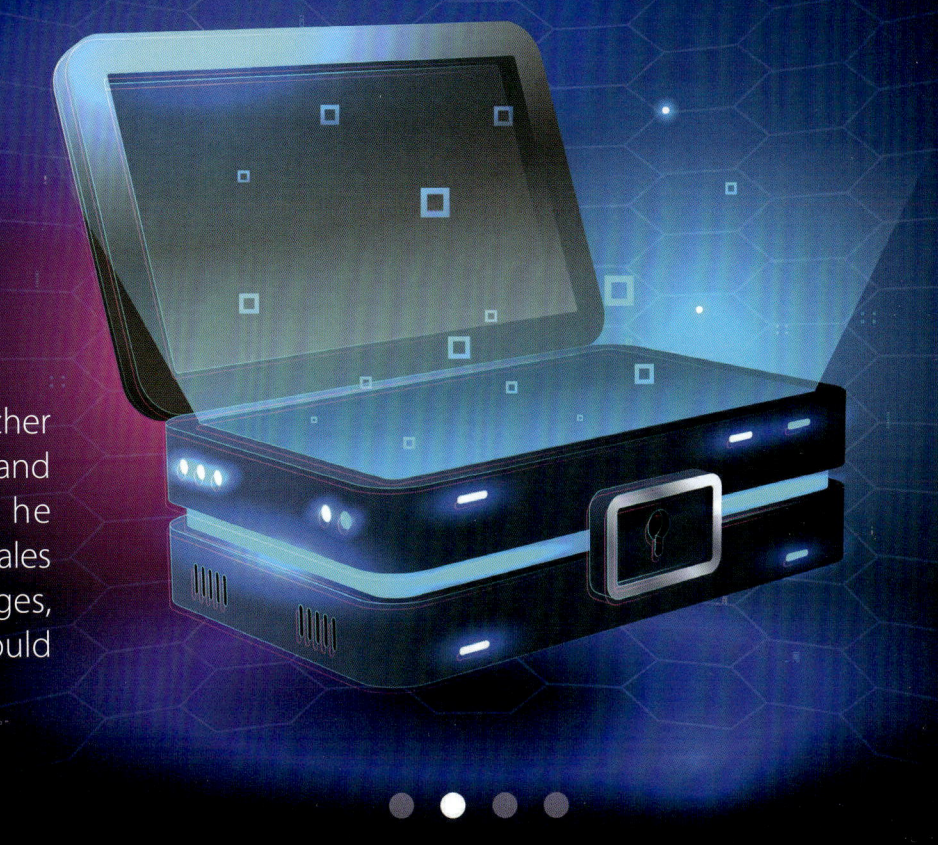

Families in the UK may be spending more than ever before on video games. Industry reports estimate that in 2021 we spent over £7 billion on gaming.

Video games afford children and their families endless opportunities for joyful, meaningful and constructive play. However, to generate these record-breaking figures, video game publishers have introduced a variety of controversial new ways to make money from gamers.

These sales tactics have led to concerns that some of the ways that video games encourage spending are similar to gambling. Indeed, gamers have reported feeling forced into spending, particularly in mobile games.

In this post, I explain how we got here – and what we should do next.

A brief history of video game monetisation

For my eighth birthday, my father bought me a game that would change my life: *Fury of the Furries*. I spent dozens of hours in Fury's small and perilous world.

The way this game's publisher made money from my play was straightforward: the game was sold as a boxed product to my father for a flat fee (say, £50). The publisher simply had to convince people to hand over £50 for the game. If enough people bought copies, the publisher would make back the money that they had spent developing, boxing and advertising it. Anything on top would be profit, but anything less would be loss.

This traditional way of selling was extremely risky. Companies put huge amounts of cash into developing each game, but only found out if they would make that money back in a brief window surrounding the game's launch. Just as box-office bombs can sink entire Hollywood studios, so did single games bankrupt entire studios with an unsuccessful launch.

This all changed with the release of 2006's *TES IV: Oblivion* (predecessor to the hugely popular *Skyrim*). In this fantasy role-playing game you can ride horses, fight monsters and learn magic. And just like *Fury of the Furries*, *Oblivion* was sold as a boxed product. To load it into your Windows PC or Xbox 360, you had to pay to own a physical disk or download the game onto your hard drive.

However, in addition, the makers offered players an additional deal. For a couple of pounds extra, they would get exclusive armour for their horse, which could not be found or won anywhere else in the game. They did not have to do anything in-game to get this armour: they just had to pay.

Players railed against this additional cost – but also bought the horse armour in droves.

Games to sales platforms

This was the birth of the microtransaction, a monetisation technique in which players repeatedly spend money for small amounts of in-game content.

Games were now no longer just products, but sales platforms, meaning publishers could continually monetise players over time.

As time went by, microtransactions became increasingly diverse and experimental. Some companies began offering players the ability to purchase in-game items and boosts that would make them perform better. Others built sophisticated, randomised reward mechanisms. After paying, players would be given a randomly-determined reward of uncertain value. It might be a rare and powerful in-game item, or a common or useless one.

These controversial reward mechanisms became known as 'loot boxes'. Loot boxes proliferated to the point that today, three-quarters of the top-grossing mobile games now contain loot boxes.

Policy has failed to keep pace

Monetisation in the video game industry has led to escalating controversies, as gamers report coercion, overspending, and serious financial impacts. Research has outlined similarities between some monetisation strategies and gambling, and shown that the more an individual spends on these microtransactions, the more likely they are to have gambling problems.

However, policy has failed to keep pace. In the UK, the presence of monetisation within a game is not tied to a set of age restrictions. Consequently, games featuring these controversial mechanisms tend to still be age-rated as suitable for children – despite the recommendations of multiple UK select committees.

It is also often not obvious from the branding of a game, making it hard for parents to make informed decisions about their child's play.

How can we safeguard play?

Policymakers, regulators and industry representatives must acknowledge that game monetisation has fundamentally changed and requires new levels of oversight and intervention. This may mean building additional data access, scrutinization and regulatory capacity into pre-existing parts of government, or the creation of a bespoke games regulator, sensitive to both the unique nature of the industry and the needs of vulnerable groups.

Video games now function as sales platforms. They should be scrutinised, restricted and regulated in a manner which takes this into account. It is only by doing this that we can ensure safe play for all.

25 August 2022

The above information is reprinted with kind permission from Parent Zone.
© 2023 Parent Zone

www.parentzone.org.uk

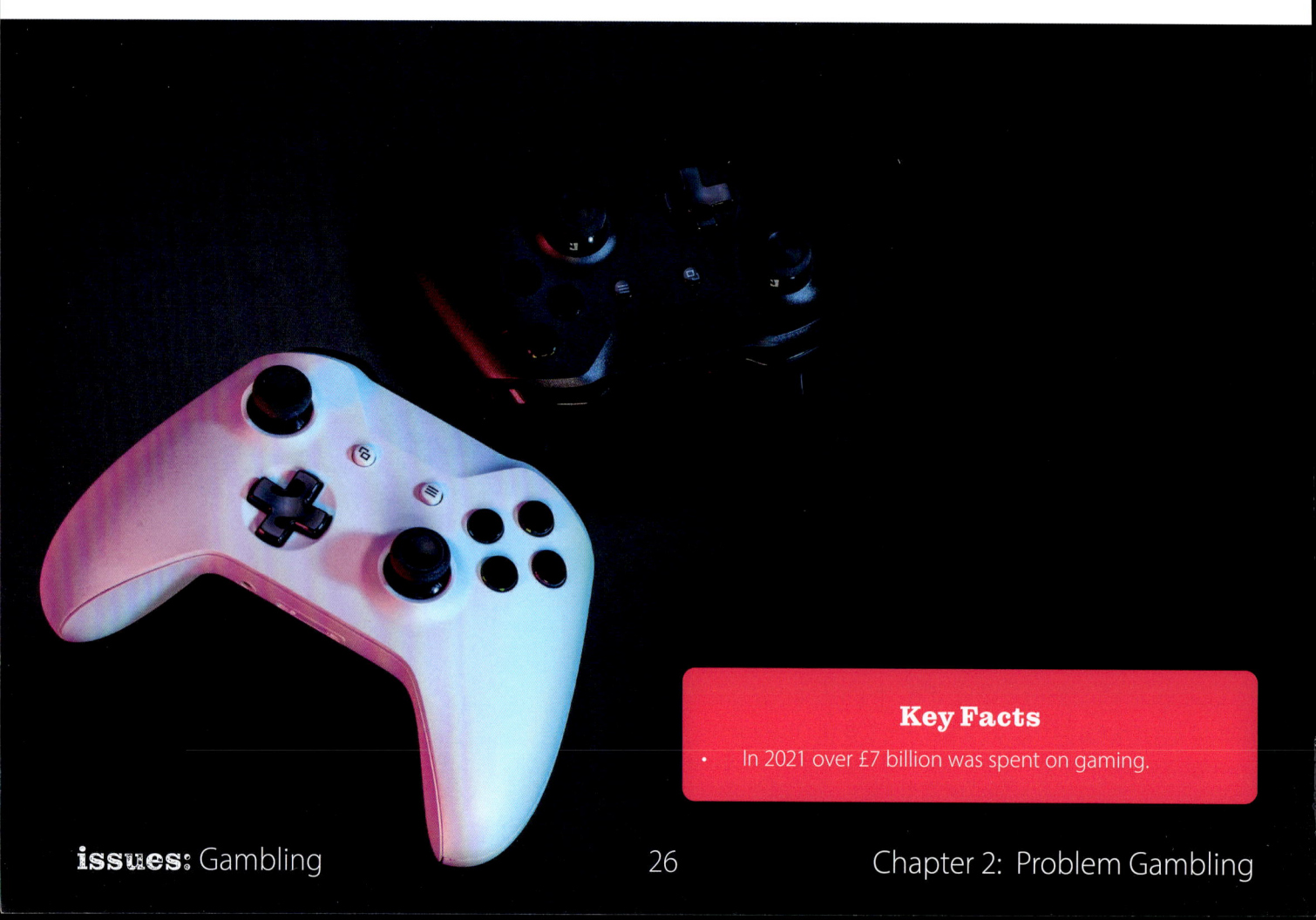

Key Facts

- In 2021 over £7 billion was spent on gaming.

Signs of gambling harm

Would you know how to spot if your own or someone else's gambling is causing harm?

Gambling is also known as the 'hidden addiction', and quite often the signs are not clear. However, from experience, we understand that these are the most common ways to identify if your own or someone else's gambling has become harmful. If you recognise these signs, we are here to support you. Our services are free, confidential and operate 24/7.

Five signs to consider about your own gambling:

1. Preoccupation – Do you spend much of your day thinking about betting? Are you finding it distracting you whilst at work, or taking you out of the moment when you spend time with friends and family? Often thinking about or planning to gamble can be one of the early warning signs that gambling could be harmful.

2. Withdrawal – Removing yourself from social and professional situations so that you can place a bet is another warning signal that your gambling might be going too far, and that the urges to gamble are potentially harming other areas of your life.

3. Escape – Life can be overwhelming at times, and you might feel like you want to escape it for a while. Using gambling as a coping mechanism is a sign of harmful gambling and can lead to losing significant amounts of money.

4. Chasing losses – The main motive of gambling is to win money but during a gambling session, that motive can change. Chasing losses is where your motive from winning money changes to winning back the money you have already lost. This can be dangerous and lead to significant losses.

5. Lying – If you find yourself hiding how much you are spending or lying about the amount of time you are gambling, or perhaps asking for money to cover bills that you are spending. These are just some signs that gambling is harming your life, and possibly risking your relationships with family and friends.

Five signs to look out for if you're concerned about someone else's gambling:

1. Withdrawn – Not wanting to join in or losing interest in usual activities or hobbies like going out with friends or spending time with family can be one of the early warning signs that gambling could be harmful. Wanting to stay at home more frequently, needing to check their phone constantly to check the latest results as so much is riding on a bet.

2. Changing mood – There could be noticeable changes to their mood and behaviour, including looking worried, agitated or upset for no apparent reason.

3. Sleeping problems – If someone is chasing losses and losing money they might not be sleeping. Anxiety or constant worrying can lead to people being up all hours. Continuing to gamble on their phone during the night could lead to sleep patterns being affected.

4. Financial signs – Has money gone missing from bank accounts, or are they regularly short of money on a regular basis and are having to borrow money? There may also be more pressure to get loans out, chasing losses now not just to generate income.

5. Lying – Are you noticing that this person is lying about what they're doing with their time, or perhaps asking for money to cover bills that could be for gambling. This can be risky as they will feel very vulnerable at being found out and very low that they have let people down.

2022

The above information is reprinted with kind permission from GamCare.
© GamCare 2023

www.gamcare.org.uk

Named and shamed: the A-listers – and football clubs – making millions from online gambling's misery

Adverts for betting firms have become commonplace in football and campaigners fear a Government u-turn could leave young fans at risk.

By Peter Stanford

It was seeing the names of betting companies on the shirts of the Tottenham Hotspur players he idolised as a teenager that first got James Grimes into gambling. That and the firms' logos all round the ground when he went there on Saturdays.

'It normalised it for me,' says the former addict whose campaign, The Big Step, aims to sever the link between football and the gambling industry. 'It corrupts the minds of young people'.

Recent reports suggest that the Government is poised to back down on its promises to take what Grimes says would be a major step towards achieving that goal. Leaks from its plan for reducing the damage done by gambling addiction indicate that it will fall short of a ban on gambling firms sponsoring the shirts of major football teams. Instead a voluntary scheme is mooted.

Why it matters, allege campaigners like Grimes and the charity Gambling With Lives, is that they believe gambling promotion around football matches and stadia is specifically designed by the industry to target vulnerable young fans and make them think that placing online bets is fun and risk-free.

Yet Public Health England in September last year reported 409 suicides in the previous 12 months linked to gambling. That is more than one every day at the same time that Britain's gambling industry, one of the world's largest, made profits of £14.2 billion in 2020.

'Fans look at the footballers in the adverts and wearing the shirts,' says former Arsenal player and recovering gambling addict Paul Merson. 'They see they are rich and think they can get rich too by gambling.'

In a recent BBC documentary Merson was especially stinging in his criticism of 'multi-millionaire' players and managers who agree to appear in gambling commercials. 'Do they need the money? Do they really need that extra £50,000?'

Jose Mourinho, Jack Wilshire, Zlatan Ibrahimovic, Harry Redknapp, Micah Richards and Roy Keane are among those who have taken the cash for on-screen endorsements. And those who know about the fees paid suggest that Merson's figure of £50,000 may be understating it.

The gambling companies for their part are tight-lipped on the sort of sums that are paid out. But one rough comparison might be the £7.5 million Hollywood A-listers Brad Pitt, Leonardo DiCaprio and Robert de Niro each reportedly earned in 2015, when they appeared in a short promotional film for the Studio City gambling complex in Macau.

However, such big-name evangelists are going to be fewer once new rules from the UK's Advertising Standards Authority kick in this October. It will ban celebrities and sporting stars from appearing in gambling adverts if they are figures who could be judged to influence the choices of young people.

Quite how that impact be measured is as yet unclear, says Will Prochaska, strategy director at Gambling With Lives. 'It won't, however, stop Skybet's name being on The Overleap, a YouTube channel where ex-England player Gary Neville interviews today's stars, or other sorts of advertisements by gambling firms appearing in teenage football magazines. Their whole business model is built on attracting the next generation of gamblers.'

Neither will it get rid of the 'loot boxes' in the sort of sports-based video games used by nearly 40 per cent of children. They allow and indeed encourage their young players to spend money on hit-or-miss in-game rewards. In Belgium, the argument that there is a link between these 'loot boxes', and young people being drawn into gambling, has been accepted by legislators who have them classified as betting products.

Yet despite a House of Lords report in 2020 suggesting that, of Britain's third of a million problem gamblers, 55,000 are children, the Government's long-awaited review of gambling legislation, promised in the 2019 Conservative election manifesto to protect young lives, will miss its target.

The Government looks likely to allow the Premier League sides that took gambling industry payments, estimated at £4-6 million each last season for short sponsorship, to continue doing so in the next. Nine out of 20 Premier League sides did so. This number will actually rise to 10 since Everton have just swapped the £9.6 million they received for shirt sponsorship last season from car dealer Cazoo in favour of 'a club-record fee', said to be as high as £12 million, to link up instead with Stake.com, one of the gambling industry's largest online operators of casinos and sports betting.

Any government-promoted voluntary scheme is going to struggle to make headway against the current run of play in football. And it is a far cry from the recommendation of the same House of Lords committee that 'no gambling advertising in or near sports grounds or sports venues' should be allowed. It highlighted that 60 per cent of the gambling industries profits came from the five per cent of gamblers with damaging addictions.

For their part most football clubs continue to argue against any such bans on commercial grounds. Rick Parry, chairman of the English Football League, has predicted that of the 72 clubs he represents, several would 'go under' if the £40 million per year they collectively earn from gambling sponsorship was lost to new Government regulations.

Yet some clubs, 20 so far, including Luton Town who came within a whisker of making it into the Premier League last season, have broken ranks and publicly signed up to The Big Step's campaign to banish gambling advertisements from their grounds.

Alongside the commercial arguments for football continuing to promote gambling are others of a more philosophical nature. They present any ban on shirt sponsorship as 'nanny-state' interference in the sort of individual liberties that some of Boris Johnson's backbench Tory MPs are keen to see the under-fire Prime Minister defending. It is being floated as one explanation for the rumoured backtracking when the report comes out.

It has been confirmed, in fairness, that the official report will contain other measures. Maximum stakes in online casinos will be set at between £2 and £5. There will be a ban on free bets and VIP packages for those with heavy losses to entice them to get in deeper.

'Non intrusive' affordability checks will be mandatory, and the regulator, the Gambling Commission, will be given more powers. A new ombudsman will hold betting firms to account for their social responsibility – though there is no mention of applying the same test to the sports stars who profit by advertising gambling.

All of which makes Ben Melvin shake his head in disappointment. A lifelong Everton fan, he has launched an online petition to change the club's mind about cosying up to Stake.com. So far over 21,000 supporters have signed up.

The 35-year-old oil refinery process operator from Ellesmere Port in Cheshire knows all too well how pernicious and damaging pro-gambling messages can be for young fans. He had begun by playing 'penny fruit machines' at 13, he says, but it was as a regular at home matches at Goodison, Everton's current stadium, that in his late teens he was drawn into heavy online gambling.

'I will never know why it took such a hold of me,' the father-of-two says, 'but I do know that the promotion and advertising of betting in sport and by sports people played its part.'

By his twenties, with his mobile phone, he had 'a casino in the palm of my hand. It was the first thing I thought about each morning and the last thing at night. When I did try to give up having a bet on the Everton match, I found I didn't even enjoy watching the football as much.'

Crippling debts and self-loathing led him to seek to break the habit. He has now gone two and a half years without gambling.

What he regrets most, Melvin says, is not the debts that he will be paying off for the rest of his life, but the lies and deceit that he used to keep his habit secret from his wife, Kelly. 'I took my family and friends down on this journey with me. I am so lucky that Kelly has stuck with me. I'm not sure if I would have.'

While he feels that the whole football establishment, including some of its biggest names, is in denial about the damage done by its links with gambling, he reserves particular anger for Everton.

'My beloved club has always prided itself on being a 'people's club', rooted in its community, supporting local people when they have problems. What it is doing now goes completely against that. It's a major step in the wrong direction when they could have taken a stance about the harm that they know gambling can do'.

The same words, he suggests, might be applied to the Government if it does, as reported, change its mind on banning football shirt sponsorship.

7 July 2022

The above information is reprinted with kind permission from *The Telegraph*.
© Telegraph Media Group Limited 2022

www.telegraph.co.uk

How UK gambling safeguards fail to defend online punters

An *Observer* investigation finds Stake.com, the Australian sponsor of Everton, could be benefiting from weak controls designed to prevent British customers betting with cryptocurrency.

By Rob Davies and Matei Rosca

When Everton FC's players ran out to face bitter Merseyside rivals Liverpool last month, their shirts were emblazoned, courtesy of a £10-million-a-year sponsorship deal, with the name Stake.com.

Until recently an obscure online betting firm, Stake.com, which specialises in controversial cryptocurrency gambling, has followed traditional bookmakers in hitching itself to the world's most popular game. And football was a keen recipient of new sponsorship revenues.

Stake has splashed plenty of cash elsewhere, too. A partnership with platinum-selling Canadian rapper Drake means his fans can watch live video streams of him gambling millions of dollars at a time. Stake has also spent big on sponsorship deals with Ultimate Fighting Championship (UFC) and Formula One driver Pietro Fittipaldi.

Stake's low-profile 27-year-old co-founder, Ed Craven, has been equally lavish, spending a combined £70 million on two mansions in the wealthy Toorak suburb of Melbourne, Australia, where Stake.com and its parent company, EasyGo, are based.

These extravagances are funded by the firm's huge annual revenue, but in theory none of it should be coming from customers gambling with digital currency in the US and UK, where this is effectively banned.

However, an investigation by the *Observer* has found that Stake.com's lucrative and fast-growing empire may be benefiting from lax controls on customers – including under-18s – betting with crypto.

Last month, the *Observer* asked Stake.com whether UK punters might be using virtual private networks (VPNs) – widely available digital tools that create a spoof location for a computer – to bypass country restrictions on crypto gambling. Stake.com said it had implemented 'stringent compliance processes' to prevent this. But in tests, these processes were found to be anything but stringent.

Using a VPN, the *Observer* was able to access Stake.com's crypto gambling services from a UK location within seconds.

When asked for age verification, reporters uploaded a photograph of a packet of Strepsils throat sweets instead of a legitimate form of ID such as driving licence or passport. This initially proved sufficient.

The reporters were then able to buy crypto via Stake.com, deposit it in a betting account, and proceed to lose the money on Stake.com's slot machine games, such as Sugar Rush and Starlight Princess. It was also able to move the remaining funds into an online bank account. They could even buy crypto with one bank account and move the funds into another account, with Stake.com effectively operating as a digital currency transfer provider.

'Reporters uploaded a photograph of a Strepsil packet as proof of age, and were initially allowed to buy crypto and bet with it on Stake.com slot machine games'

It took more than 48 hours for Stake.com to suspend the account, after spotting that a Strepsils packet was not proof of adulthood. While the company eventually cracked down on the fake ID, subsequent tests suggest an approved adult could have continued gambling with crypto, even though the Gambling Commission has yet to give any operator approval to offer such a product in the UK.

There is reason to believe that VPN crypto gambling may be vulnerable to those seeking to bet using the proceeds of crime. According to the website reporter.london, an unnamed crypto trading platform is preparing to sue Stake.com, claiming that one of its traders stole £350,000 of the digital currency ethereum and gambled it away on Stake, using VPNs.

Asked about the *Observer's* test crypto bets, Stake.com said: 'As with all companies in the sector, Stake.com experiences unauthorised users attempting to evade geoblocking through VPNs. Stake is aware of one account that was recently opened following the use of a VPN from the UK and the submission of false address and other false user information, all in violation of the company's terms of service. This account was detected by Stake's internal compliance processes and shut down.

'Stake.com utilises anti-money laundering measures on its site. Fiat to cryptocurrency exchange services are offered by third-party providers (not Stake.com), who also have their own compliance processes and requirements.' The company also offered assurances about its commitment to safer gambling.

However, one of Stake.com's most important commercial partnerships is with xQc, a Canadian internet personality whose real name is Félix Lengyel, who has more than 11 million followers on the live video platform Twitch.

With his bombastic style and machine-gun-fire speech, Lengyel, who is 25, regularly attracts tens of thousands of viewers at a time to his streams, in which he gambles on Stake.com slot machines.

Lengyel has repeatedly stated that he is addicted to gambling, and at one stage even pledged to stop making slot machine video streams. Yet, after a brief period away from the world of betting, he signed a deal with Stake.com and returned to the fray in 2022.

Under the terms of his deal, Lengyel gets a cut when people click through to the Stake.com site via his Twitch channel.

He claimed earlier this year to have funnelled $119 million in bets to the company.

Like all licensed operators, Stake.com does not allow under-18s to gamble. Until now, however, anyone over 13 can watch xQc's streams on Twitch. Last month, Twitch decided to ban casino and slots streams from its platform, naming Stake.com as one of the operators whose games it would no longer help promote. This was in response to threats from prominent streamers, some of whom had watched in horror as gambling streams began to overtake video gaming as the site's main output.

So that was a key marketing tool lost, but Stake.com still has its high-profile sponsorship deals, including with English football teams Everton and Watford.

These deals are possible via controversial but legal 'white-label' deals, under which a foreign brand that wants a presence in Britain can piggy-back on to a licence already held by a local operator, without going through its own licensing process.

Stake's white-label deal is with Isle of Man-based TGP Europe, a business that is also the entry point for Leeds United sponsor SBOTOP, a Philippines-based online bookie, and Hull City's deal with Kenyan-owned SportPesa. The arrangement allows Stake to offer gambling services with fiat currency (normal money) but not crypto, in the UK.

White labels are a backdoor used by some of the little-known betting firms that sponsor English football teams. The deals allow them to reach the eyeballs of football-watching punters in markets such as China and Thailand, where gambling is theoretically illegal and cannot be promoted.

But there are also questions about whether foreign firms are avoiding a moral obligation to help tackle gambling addiction in the UK. One important way in which large licensed operators such as Ladbrokes and Bet365 do this is by paying 0.1% of their winnings as a voluntary levy to the GambleAware charity.

But Stake.com is not technically the licensed operator; TGP Europe is. And last year TGP paid £2,000 to GambleAware, which would implying that its revenue was just £2 million. And GambleAware's list of donors does not mention Stake.com.

'White labels allow companies like Stake to avoid the due diligence of a licensing process, allowing them to advertise and access the British market,' said Matt Zarb-Cousin of campaign group Clean Up Gambling.

'All gambling firms should have to apply for a full licence if they want to legitimately operate here. The Gambling Commission and DCMS [Department for Digital, Culture, Media and Sport] should not be endorsing the white-label system, which privileges those unwilling to go through the licensing process.'

The Gambling Commission said: 'If there is evidence that a gambling company that is not licensed by us is knowingly allowing British consumers to gamble then we would want that evidence provided to us so we can consider appropriate action.'

Even if Stake.com did acquire its own licence to operate in Britain, there is no guarantee that it would have much to fear from the regulator.

In August, the Guardian reported that Everton FC told Stake.com to stop using club branding in a promotion that offered a $10 free bet to anyone who wagered $5,000 in a month.

It was not a matter for the Gambling Commission though. The offer may have been cloaked in the imagery of a 144-year-old stalwart of English football but it was priced in dollars and, ostensibly, unavailable to British punters – except those who knew how to use a VPN, that is.

1 October 2022

The above information is reprinted with kind permission from *The Guardian*.
© 2023 Guardian News and Media Limited

www.theguardian.com

issues: Gambling · 31 · Chapter 2: Problem Gambling

Football Index's collapse reveals a deeper rot in UK gambling industry

Customers are estimated to have lost £90 million, showing why proper regulation is more essential than ever, says John Lubbock.

By John Lubbock

The UK's gambling industry is worth £14.4 billion a year and has produced some of the country's richest CEOs, but last week's collapse of Football Index (FI) – an opaque gambling product which marketed itself as a 'football stock market' – is now raising questions about whether the industry is so unregulated that it has become a Wild West enterprise, exploiting vulnerable people with little oversight.

FI's users were encouraged to invest in what the company advertised as a stock market – often by friends and family who earned money as 'affiliates' of the company, receiving commission for attracting new users. There is now widespread anger among punters who cannot be sure that they will get any of their money back, with *The Times* estimating customer losses of £90 million.

Advertising for online gambling products seems to have expanded significantly during the Coronavirus pandemic, with betting shops closed. FI appeared to be a highly dubious gambling product, which appealed to men who believed their superior knowledge of football could give them a competitive edge.

But the pandemic also created a big problem for FI. The suspension of football matches would inevitably have a knock-on effect on FI share prices, with footballers out of the news and not playing games.

FI did not have the characteristics of a market, because its owners could change the rules whenever they wanted. The spread between the 'buy' and 'sell' price for players was also so wide that it was almost impossible to make any profit. For example, Harry Kane could be sold at £4.15 but bought at £6.91, while Lionel Messi could be sold at £2.95 and bought at £4.91.

There was also 2% commission on sales, mopped up by FI. To sweeten the deal, it paid out 'dividends' on shares on players receiving significant media attention.

The Advertising Standards Authority (ASA) upheld a complaint in 2019 that an advert for the site was misleading. It said 'the impression created by the ad was for a product that was an investment opportunity when, in fact, it was a betting product and did not make the associated financial risks clear, and concluded that it was irresponsible and breached the code'.

FI's terms and conditions stated that it used 'an algorithm to determine share price changes. From time to time, we may change our algorithm to accommodate changes in market dynamics and scale'.

Last June, I emailed FI asking it about how the site worked. To what extent were the buy and sell prices effectively independent of its control? In response, FI referred to the help section of its website.

In September, FI was awarded second place on the *Sunday Times* 'Sage Tech Track 100', which 'ranks Britain's 100 private tech companies with the fastest-growing sales over their latest three years'. FI received this accolade because the firm 'paid out double cash dividends to its traders during lockdown'. At this point, the company boasted of having more than 500,000 users.

In December, amid a wave of FI share price crashes, the company's CEO Adam Cole announced that he would be stepping down. Cole and current FI CEO Michael Bolan are still listed as directors of FI's parent company, Index Labs Ltd, though three of the company's directors have left since the end of January this year and the company doesn't seem to have filed accounts since 2019.

Earlier this month, FI posted a 'market update' to its website – announcing that cash dividends on shares in players were being slashed. These dividends were an important part of encouraging users to continue gambling and cutting them was the final straw for many. Portfolio prices collapsed, and the chorus of people openly suggesting that this gambling product resembled a Ponzi Scheme began to grow.

On 11 March, the Gambling Commission finally stepped in, removing the company's license to operate. The administrators were called.

Billions and bust

These actions were far too little and too late, however.

The warning signs had been there since at least the middle of last year. The crash in share prices began last September, with users unable to sell their shares, effectively locked into their portfolios, watching their values crash.

Caan Berry, a professional sports trader who raised concerns about FI's model on his YouTube channel, was then subjected to a campaign of abuse by users of the site. Berry had asked a number of questions about FI's changes to its rules, including the removal of an 'instant sell' feature which allowed users to sell shares back to the company.

Brian Chappell, of the group Justice For Punters (J4P), had been sending the Gambling Commission (GC) information about the underlying problems with FI. He believes that the Commission should use experienced gamblers as consultants. One of J4P's volunteers, who applied to work at the GC, was turned down for a job because he gambled.

'When someone comes along with a new product like this, they don't really have anybody in the building who knows what it's really about,' he says.

'The only thing the GC have done since they first started getting complaints, I'm talking about a long time ago now, is they made [FI] put on their website right at the top, that this is betting, because before that they had definitely marketed it as "you can make money out of your football knowledge".'

For Chappell, 'what the GC didn't pick up was that these shares, eventually, may have no real value. You were not buying into the player, and you were buying them off a company who were able to print new shares virtually at will, thus affecting supply and demand, and having a negative effect on price... What you're doing is trading in individual player markets where the number of shares is changing, so where players at some point may become worthless.'

Chappell says that the GC has always been under pressure to 'regulate with a light touch'. Following the Gambling Act of 2005, massive corporations have taken over the gambling industry in the UK and have asked regulators to allow them to self-regulate. Chappell says that the Financial Conduct Authority should have been called in to look at FI.

If the GC had frozen the assets of FI at the end of last year, consumers would have been given a chance to retrieve some of their money, which seems unlikely now. Other bodies such as the Competition and Markets Authority and the Department of Digital, Culture, Media and Sport (DCMS) could have intervened, but ultimately did nothing.

The Gambling Commission did not reply to *Byline Times*' request for comment but, in a response to The Athletic, said that 'people using gambling operators do so at their own risk' and that 'we do not oversee their businesses on a day-to-day basis or monitor the financial health of operators directly in real-time. That would impose significant regulatory costs and could give a false sense of security to customers'.

Neil McArthur, head of the Gambling Commission, resigned with immediate effect on Monday morning. *The Guardian* reported that McArthur's departure is 'understood to be unrelated to' FI's collapse, though the timing raises more questions than it answers. Football Index users are now planning a class action lawsuit against the firm, though this may be complicated by the company being registered offshore in Jersey.

The wider picture is of a gambling industry taking advantage of deregulation that allows it to make billions of pounds a year with little oversight or intervention from regulators. The Conservative Party has also received millions of pounds in donations from betting company owners such as Stuart Wheeler over the past 20 years.

Chappell says that, although the 2005 Gambling Act is being reviewed, 'it's already clear that gambling industry lobbyists have obtained regular access to the DCMS to campaign for their paymasters'.

Football Index has been exposed as an unworkable and exploitative product, but its collapse does not stop other, more traditional forms of gambling from continuing to make huge profits, which amount to a large-scale transfer of wealth from the poor to the rich.

It is clearly time for more regulation and for reform of the Gambling Commission at the very least – although, sadly, it is doubtful that this Government will listen.

FI did not respond to *Byline Times*' request for comment.

18 March 2021

Key Facts

- The UK's gambling industry is worth £14.4 billion a year.
- It is estimated Football Index customers lost in the region of £90 million following its collapse.

Write

What is a Ponzi Scheme? Write a short paragraph describing what it is.

The above information is reprinted with kind permission from *Byline Times*.
© 2023 Byline Media Holdings Ltd, Byline Times & Yes We Work Ltd

www.bylinetimes.com

Match-fixing an increasing threat as global sports betting turnover surpasses €1.45 trillion for the first time

Sportradar Integrity Services has revealed the detection of a record number of suspicious matches in its annual 'Betting Corruption and Match-fixing' report.

Sportradar's bet-monitoring service, the Universal Fraud Detection System (UFDS), identified 903 matches in 2021 which showed signs of suspicious activity, across 10 sports and in 76 countries.

This represents the highest number of suspicious matches recorded in Sportradar Integrity Services' 17-year history and a 2.4 per cent increase on the previous high of 882 suspicious matches recorded in 2019.

As well as an increase in suspicious activity, record levels of global sports betting turnover were recorded, which Sportradar now estimates at more than €1.45 trillion. According to the report, in 2021 approximately €165 million was generated in match-fixing betting profit.

In response to the record number of suspicious matches, Sportradar worked with its partners to support 65 sanctions: 46 sporting sanctions, 15 criminal sanctions and four sanctions that were both sporting and criminal. These were delivered in 11 countries across football and tennis, with lifetime bans handed down to eight athletes.

'There is no easy short-term solution to the match-fixing issue, and we're likely to see similar numbers of suspicious matches in 2022, if not more,' said Sportradar Integrity Services managing director Andreas Krannich. 'As the market has developed, so the threat of match fixing has evolved. Now, would-be corruptors take an increasingly direct approach to match-fixing and betting corruption, with athletes messaged directly via social-media platforms.

'We can take what we observed in 2021 and ask ourselves as fans of sport, what lessons can we learn? At Sportradar, we believe in adopting a progressive approach to integrity protection, through bet monitoring and intelligence gathering. This has been proven to deliver sanctions against those involved in match-fixing. Preventative measures, such as educating athletes and stakeholders, are also crucially important in the long-term fight against match-fixing.'

Soccer had the highest frequency of suspicious matches last year at a rate of one in every 201 fixtures, followed by eSports with one in every 384, and basketball at one in 498.

September and October 2021 saw the highest number of suspicious matches detected with 105 and 104, respectively. This corresponds with the start of the traditional soccer season.

Sunday is the most common day of the week for suspicious sporting fixtures to occur, accounting for 22.5 per cent of all cases, followed by Wednesday at 16.8 per cent and Saturday at 15.6 per cent, reflecting the large number of soccer matches played on these days of the week.

The report forecasts a further increase in the number of suspicious matches in 2022.

Sportradar made the UFDS available free of charge to all sports globally in October 2021, in an effort to ensure clean sport and to support all sports at all levels with their integrity measures. The system is used by more than 120 sports organisations globally, including large international federations such as FIFA, UEFA, ITF, and ICC through to smaller organisations representing an individual sport in a single country.

4 March 2022

The above information is reprinted with kind permission from Gaming Intelligence.
© 2023 Gaming Intelligence Services Ltd

www.gamingintelligence.com

Solutions

Chapter 3

NHS launches new gambling addiction clinics to meet record demand

Two new gambling clinics will open in England this year, the NHS announced today as it faces record demand for specialist support for gambling addiction.

The two new clinics, based in Southampton and Stoke-On-Trent, will open from May and mean there will be seven specialist clinics in place across England.

The other five NHS gambling addiction clinics in London, Leeds, Manchester, Sunderland and a national children and young person's pilot clinic will inform the rollout of further gambling clinics when the services are evaluated later this year.

The north of England has the highest prevalence of at-risk gamblers, with 4.4% of adults in the North West and 4.9% in the North East being at the most risk of addiction.

Between April and December last year, 668 people with the most severe gambling addiction issues were referred to NHS gambling clinics – up from 575 during the same period in 2020 – a 16.2% increase.

The news comes alongside a letter from NHS mental health chief Claire Murdoch to GambleAware, confirming that the NHS will be fully funding its own gambling services from April – bringing the support in line with other NHS services.

The decision follows feedback from patients and clinicians opposing the conflict of interest from the gambling industry, which generates profits of over £14 billion a year in the UK, in funding treatment for addiction.

Research published by Public Health England (now the UK Health Security Agency) last September estimated around 0.5% of the adult population, around 246,000 people, are likely to have some form of gambling addiction with around 2.2 million people either problem gamblers or at risk of addiction.

NHS mental health director Claire Murdoch said: 'Gambling addiction is a cruel mental health condition that can devastate people's lives – our pilot clinics are already having a lasting impact in helping people to take back vital control of their lives.

'The opening of two new gambling clinics in May, as a part of our £2.3 billion investment into mental health services, will mean we can help even more people with the most serious gambling problems.

'It is also absolutely right that the NHS now funds these clinics independently, recognising the harmful effects this addiction can have on the nation's mental health, and that predatory tactics from gambling companies are part of the problem, not the solution'.

Later this year the NHS will launch a new Gambling Harm Network and Clinical Reference Group, which will bring expertise together and enable clinical teams to share best practices for helping to treat gambling addiction.

Gambling addiction if it takes hold can destroy lives. Nick Firth, aged 31 from West Yorkshire, struggled with a gambling addiction for 12 years. Feeling ashamed to admit he had a problem, the addiction also took over his life to the extent he would beg, borrow, and steal money to fund it, straining relationships with family and friends.

Nick finally reached out for help from NHS gambling services during the peak of his addiction in January last year, when he felt suicide was the only way out. With his own NHS support worker, Nick underwent group cognitive behavioural therapy to help treat his addiction and as a result, hasn't gambled since.

Nick said: 'Gambling addiction took over my life to the extent I was suicidal and relationships with my family and friends had broken down.

'The team at the NHS gambling addiction service have helped completely turn my life around, engaging with NHS services is one of the best things I've ever done – it's helped me get control of my life back and I'm rebuilding trust with my family and friends, once again having happy and healthy relationships with people close to me.

'Anybody out there who is struggling with addiction should know they are not alone, while there is no quick fix, there is help out there that can help treat your addiction and seeking help is the best thing you can do to help yourself get better'.

In January 2020, NHS mental health director Claire Murdoch wrote to gambling companies outlining actions they should take to improve the odds for people struggling with addiction. Other than the restriction of bets taken by credit cards, implemented when the Gambling Commission outlawed the practice, the gambling industry continues to offer customers VIP packages and streams live sports, all of which can be potentially harmful to those struggling with addiction.

25 April 2022

The above information is reprinted with kind permission from the NHS.
© Crown Copyright 2023
This information is licensed under the Open Government Licence v3.0
To view this licence, visit http://www.nationalarchives.gov.uk/doc/open-government-licence/

www.england.nhs.uk

issues: Gambling   35   Chapter 3: Solutions

Gambling needs more holistic management to reduce harm when it causes debt, new research suggests

Gambling treatment and support services need to dovetail better with debt advice, to ensure recovery pathways for people affected by gambling harm are more likely to succeed, according to a new report by the University of Bristol.

The report in partnership with StepChange Debt Charity, supported by the Gambling Commission, finds gambling is only rarely reported as a driver of problem debt, with around 2% of StepChange clients disclosing gambling associated with their debt.

However, gambling debt can be deeply harmful when it does occur and can badly affect not just the individual, but also others close to them. This is especially true if continued use of credit to fund gambling leads to other bills going unpaid, potentially putting homes and wider household finances at significant risk. The research finds that those affected by someone else's gambling often go unseen, and there is more to do to ensure these clients are effectively supported.

The new report suggests it is incumbent on gambling firms, credit providers and the advice sector to recognise the specific problems those with extensive gambling debt can face, and the challenges and opportunities to address when seeking to resolve them.

Based on an analysis of 206,241 client data records and interviews with 30 StepChange clients, authors Sara Davies, Jamie Evans and Professor Sharon Collard find that there are some notable profile differences between those affected by gambling-related debt and the wider population of StepChange clients.

Clients who disclosed a gambling problem to StepChange were more likely to be male (71% compared with 40% of all clients) and had higher average annual incomes (median income £18,000 compared with £15,470 for other clients). They also had higher unsecured debts (£1,250 higher in Q1-2 2021), and lower arrears (£2,178 in arrears compared with £2,791 for other clients). They experienced less enforcement action (5.5% faced bailiff action compared with 9.2% all clients).

A common factor in the interviewees' histories is that gambling was facilitated by taking on consumer credit debt. Two other common threads were the pandemic lockdowns as a trigger for gambling escalation; and the incentives offered by gambling operators as a motivation for gambling.

For most of the clients interviewed, gambling was the primary or sole reason for their debt problems. Typically, they had used consumer credit - overdrafts, personal loans, and credit cards (prior to the April 2020 ban on using credit cards for bets) - to fund gambling, to the point where all lines of credit were exhausted. This accounts for the high levels of unsecured consumer credit debt seen in the client data.

Another cause of problem debt, especially among those affected by another person's gambling, stemmed from using consumer credit to fill the financial hole left by gambling to keep household finances afloat, because the person gambling was spending their earnings on gambling. Secrecy was often a defining feature in the production of gambling-related debt. This could result in significant delays in people seeking advice, which in turn impacted the options open to them by the time they did.

Professor Sharon Collard, Research Director of the University of Bristol's Personal Finance Research Centre, said: 'Gambling-related debt is a serious issue that can lead to relationship problems, physical and mental health problems, and even crime. Our landmark study is an important step forward in understanding how gambling and problem debt are linked.

'Given our evidence about the complementary and mutually reinforcing benefits of debt advice and gambling treatment and support, it may be time to consider whether debt advice should be routinely funded as part of gambling treatment and support interventions and programmes. The experiences of the debt advice clients we spoke to also confirms the urgent need for measures to ensure gambling operators prevent significant financial harm occurring among their customers.'

Peter Tutton, Head of Policy, Research and Public Affairs at StepChange Debt Charity, added: 'Gambling can suck people into a compulsive cycle that can be incredibly financially damaging to them, and potentially to their loved ones too. As this research shows, vulnerability due to gambling is complex, and can need more than debt advice to fix on a permanent basis.

'Gambling firms and consumer credit lenders need to try to spot and deal with warning signs earlier, while the debt advice sector needs to continue to develop holistic ways of working with other advice and support services that people with gambling vulnerability need, alongside their debt advice. We'll be seeking to work on practical ways to achieve these results, on the basis of the insights gained from the report.'

Tim Miller, Executive Director of Research and Policy at the Gambling Commission, said: 'Ongoing research into gambling harms has always been hugely vital to help understand the causes and the trends, and also establish ways to address those harms.

'This latest study utilises data from StepChange in a new way to help better understand the role of gambling in consumer debt, and importantly, where certain organisations and their experts can link in with each other. It provides another addition to the wider evidence base which as the industry regulator we welcome.'

18 October 2022

Key Facts

- A report in partnership with StepChange Debt Charity, supported by the Gambling Commission, found that only 2% of clients disclose gambling as a contributing factor to their debt.
- In April 2020 the use of credit cards to place bets was banned.

Research

Do some research into the effect gambling can have on people's lives. You should consider the financial, social and mental health impact when it becomes an addiction. Write a report on your findings and feedback to your class.

The above information is reprinted with kind permission from University of Bristol.
© 2002-2023 University of Bristol

www.bristol.ac.uk

Supporting schools to tackle and prevent gambling harms

A new framework is designed to help teachers and leaders approach the growing concern of gambling harms with confidence, writes Jane Rigbye.

Teachers are coming to us more and more seeking support to talk about gambling. That's a good thing. It's in part due to gambling being included in the new PSHE curriculum introduced last year. But there are other reasons too.

In 2019, the Gambling Commission estimated that as many as 350,000 11-to-16-year-olds were spending their own money on gambling each week, that 55,000 young people in that bracket were experiencing social or emotional difficulties due to their gambling, and that a further 87,000 were 'at risk' of doing so.

Britain is home to one of the largest online gambling markets in the world and is one of the only jurisdictions where some forms of gambling can be legally participated in by those under the age of 18. So while most regulated gambling products such as the National Lottery, online gambling and sports betting are restricted to over 18s, it would be naïve to think young people are unfamiliar with gambling prior to entering legal adulthood. Therefore, it is more important than ever that we work together to safeguard our future generations from potential gambling harms.

Gambling disorder has been recognised by the World Health Organization as an addictive behaviour, and online gambling marketing is listed alongside marketing of fast food and sugar-sweetened drinks as an unhealthy commodity, which can harm relationships, school achievement and mental health.

However, gambling disorder is complex and it's sometimes known as the hidden addiction because it can be difficult to spot the signs of harm. Looking out for changes in a young person's behaviour, ensuring they have a strong support network and monitoring their actions can help identify issues sooner.

Common emotional harms include individuals becoming more secretive, stressed, and withdrawn. The impact of gambling on a young person's mental health might result in them struggling to focus or disengaging from normal life. Physical signs of harm include fatigue, headaches, borrowing money and money going missing. These are signs we should all recognise.

'We don't hesitate to talk with children about other risky behaviour'

We don't hesitate to talk with children about the risks associated with other behaviours such as consuming alcohol, tobacco, or drugs. Our conversations in schools – formal and informal, in lessons, assemblies and on the playground – can help inform young people about the risks of gambling.

We engage with the education sector daily. Although the new PSHE curriculum is an encouraging step forward, teachers tell us they need resources to help them address the issue more than ever. What's more, we know this is not an issue that can be visited only once during a child's time at secondary school. Knowledge needs to be built over time and reinforced regularly.

But teachers are busy and the curriculum is already loaded. We shouldn't expect every teacher to become a gambling harms prevention specialist as well as everything else, but we can help them approach the issue with more confidence. That's why we have worked with GamCare and Fast Forward to produce the Gambling Education Framework – a practical, evidence-based resource launched last week.

The framework's principles have been developed in line with PSHE Association guidance on effective preventative education. It is designed to help teachers deliver high-quality teaching about gambling and manage the difficult conversations that can arise in schools. It will be just as useful for designated safeguarding leads who might have to help pupils who have a gambling problem, or who might be impacted by someone with a gambling disorder at home.

We know education is an invaluable protective measure against gambling harms, just as it is against other dangers young people are exposed to. But teachers must be equipped with the knowledge, resources and confidence to talk about the issue. We hope our framework helps to fill that gap.

11 October 2022

The above information is reprinted with kind permission from SCHOOLS WEEK.
© 2023 Schools Week

www.schoolsweek.co.uk

'Stop promoting them': victims call for football to end tragic link with gambling

Campaign to end advertising in the sport organising walk in memory of loved ones lost to gambling-related suicides.

By John Brewin

Kimberly Wadsworth was 32 when she took her own life in 2018. The passionate Leeds fan who worked in marketing was a gambling addict. Having begun on the fixed-odds betting terminals found in any high-street bookmaker she had graduated to online casinos.

There she was plied with 'free' bets and gained VIP status from the companies she gambled with. They incentivised her to keep playing even when her losses were heavy. Hers is a not unfamiliar story – Public Health England estimates there are 409 gambling- related suicides each year in England – but she is a reminder that gambling addiction is not an exclusively male affliction.

On Friday and Saturday, Kimberly's mother, Kay, will join recovering gambling addicts and other families who have lost loved ones to gambling-related suicide in walking to five Yorkshire football grounds, starting with an early appointment at Sheffield Wednesday's Hillsborough. From there the group of more than 30 will visit Sheffield United's Bramall Lane, Rotherham's New York Stadium and Barnsley's Oakwell.

On Saturday, the group take the 19 miles from Barnsley to Leeds to complete 41 miles over two days. They have been allowed by club officials to take pictures inside Elland Road. 'I am proud to walk in Kimberly's memory with people who have suffered the harm and devastation that gambling addiction brings,' said Kay. 'These harmful gambling products are designed to hook people in, regardless of their background, so we are calling on football to stop promoting them to millions of young fans.'

The event is the latest organised by the Big Step, a campaign to end gambling advertising and sponsorship in football, led by people harmed by gambling. Previous events include July's 70-person walk from Manchester to Liverpool in memory of Ryan Myers, a 27-year-old Liverpool-supporting carpenter. In February, a three-day hike took in Scottish stadiums on the route from Edinburgh to Glasgow in remembrance of Lewis Keogh, a 34-year-old Sheffield Wednesday fan.

This weekend's walk's aim is highlighting, in the words of James Grimes, the organiser and Big Step founder, that 'this is not just a male issue. Although football was a part of Kimberly's addiction so were other parts of gambling that you wouldn't necessarily associate with a young, male football fan.'

Football club shirts, websites, social media, pitchside banners and in particular TV advertising continue to be awash with gambling, despite lobbying that aims to protect young eyes from being enticed. Grimes is a recovering addict whose 12-year journey from football betting as a 16-year-old Tottenham fan took in about 50 gambling companies across myriad betting products including online casinos to the point of being 'basically suicidal' after a heavy losing run on a fixed-odds betting terminal.

'Spurs had a casino on the front of their shirts at that time: Mansion. That was a company I went on to use and it quickly consumed all of my life. Football was a constant in it. Whenever I saw new companies pop up on shirts or the side of the pitch, I would use those sites. It sucked everything away from me. I turned from a happy, normal boy into a hopeless, helpless wreck of a man.

'The thing I try to emphasise is that it was only gambling that did that. I had a great upbringing, there was no trauma, I never had an addiction to anything else.'

Grimes believes he fell victim to the liberalised 2005 Gambling Act that opened up the flood of betting advertising. From there, the 18-25 market, especially vulnerable, was exposed to a cornucopia of gambling products in which football bets became a gateway drug towards becoming the VIP clients companies take heavy profit from.

Could things be changing? Of the five Yorkshire clubs visited by the Big Step this weekend, only one, Leeds, has a betting shirt sponsor, the Manx-based SBOTOP. Barnsley began the season with a rapidly curtailed cryptocurrency deal, a reminder of clubs' eternal attraction to easy money. When the Big Step campaign began in 2019, 28 of 44 Premier League and Championship clubs had betting shirt sponsors, a number now reduced to 14.

Despite heavy lobbying and growing resistance among fans, betting advertising pervades on TV, radio and the web. A government white paper on gambling reform was postponed for a fourth time in July. The presence in government of the anti-gambling advocate Chris Philp, chief secretary to the Treasury, and the influence of Iain Duncan Smith, similarly minded, in Liz Truss's leadership campaign are yet to be brought to bear. For now, football clubs continue to act as advertising boards for an industry held responsible for the loss of Kimberly and many others.

13 October 2022

The above information is reprinted with kind permission from *The Guardian*.
© 2023 Guardian News and Media Limited

www.theguardian.com

Five steps to self-care if you gamble

By guest blogger Verity

Self-care is about doing small things to take care of our own mental health. It could be taking a walk, reading a book or just having a chat with a friend. It can help you manage many situations in life, especially those which you may find difficult to deal with.

Gambling can be fun, but it also has the potential to cause harm. Gambling should also never become a way to help you deal with anything else in life you don't feel able to cope with. The tips below can help you reduce your risk of harm, and protect your mental health if you gamble.

1. Set yourself a goal

Goal setting can be effective at changing unhealthy behaviours, so if there is something you want to change, make a plan.

To become an effective goal-setter try these five steps next time you're trying to achieve something – anything!

- Put your goal in writing
- Be specific
- Make it challenging, but keep it attainable
- Make sure you're committed
- Get feedback, or reflect on your progress regularly

2. Find a hobby

If you find yourself gambling more, perhaps as a way to escape from something else, focusing your mind on other activities can help.

Try out a range of positive activities whilst using a mood tracker app – this will help you figure out what activities work best for you. Some ideas include:

- Sports/Dancing
- Playing an instrument or writing music
- Photography, painting or drawing
- Walking outside, getting closer to nature in nearby parks/woods Helping others – volunteering can help you too
- Cooking/Baking

3. Keep a diary or journal

There are lots of different ways to manage your mental health, mood, and self-esteem. Keeping a record of how you feel in the form of a diary can be particularly helpful, and may help you identify what your 'triggers' are for certain emotions or behaviours (both positive and negative).

Here are three types of diaries or journals you could keep, either on paper, online or through a dedicated app:

- **Mood diaries:** Tracking how you feel over time can help you increase your awareness of your emotions and look for patterns. If there is something that makes you feel better, you can try to incorporate more of that into your day, and if there is something that makes you feel worse you can try to reduce that.

- **Self-esteem diaries:** These encourage positive journaling, which has been found to help create feelings of well-being and self-esteem.

- **Gratitude diaries:** Gratitude can take only a few minutes a day but can have a significant impact on your life. Giving thanks can change your outlook and make your approach to life more positive overall – it may help problems feel more manageable too. There are scientifically proven benefits to developing an 'attitude of gratitude' such as enhancing empathy and reduces aggression, strengthening relationships as you notice more of the positive things people do, and improving self-esteem. Taking a minute to find the good can help your mental health significantly – try writing down three things you're grateful for, big or small, at the end of every day

4. Money management

If you gamble, a top tip to do it safely is to set a time limit and a budget that you can stick to.

Before deciding to gamble, or buy loot boxes, you'll need to know exactly what you can spend and when helping to reduce the low moments you might feel when you don't have money. Once you've budgeted for all the important things, you'll work out how much you can afford to gamble with, bearing in mind you're more likely to lose this than you are to win! When you take control of your finances, you'll generally feel in control and better able to enjoy the activities you take part in.

Write

Imagine you are an agony aunt/uncle and have received a letter from a young person who has a problem with gambling. They are spending all their money from their part-time job on gambling and have even taken money from their parents without consent. They are very worried they will be found out and what the consequences will be. They want to stop gambling but don't know how. Write a suitable reply and supply information about where they can get help.

5. Set yourself boundaries

This is something that many people of all ages struggle with, but with some practice, you can develop this skill and it will be critical to your success. Boundaries are personal, and they help you protect the things that are important to you – e.g. time with your family, your personal development, time to do things you enjoy etc.

Setting boundaries at school, work, and home helps to keep your relationships positive, reduces how much peer pressure impacts you, and helps you to stop engaging with activities when you're running on empty. Set limits on things that you can tolerate, check-in with yourself and how you're feeling about different interactions and allow yourself to take care of yourself, guilt-free. If something is making you uncomfortable, putting boundaries in place – verbally, with others too – can also help us prevent unwanted habits such as gambling problems.

By practising these self-care tips you should be able to enhance your mental health and reduce the risk of harm through gambling.

4 February 2021

The above information is reprinted with kind permission from Big Deal
© 2023 Big Deal

www.bigdeal.org.uk

Where can I find help?

Below are some telephone numbers, email addresses and websites of agencies or charities that can offer support or advice if you, or someone you know, needs it.

Be Gamble Aware
National Gambling Helpline: 0808 8020 133
www.begambleaware.co.uk

Betknowmore
Helpline: 0800 066 4827
www.betknowmoreuk.org

Gamblers Anonymous (UK)
www.gamblersanonymous.org.uk

Gam Anon & Gam Anon Scotland
www.gamanon.org.uk

Gamcare
Helpline: 0808 8020 133
www.gamcare.org.uk

Gordon Moody Association
www.gordonmoody.org.uk

StepChange Debt Charity
Helpline: 0800 138 1111
www.stepchange.org

National Gambling Helpline
0808 802 0133

Useful Websites

www.bigdeal.org.uk

www.bristol.ac.uk

www.bylinetimes.com

www.england.nhs.uk

www.gamcare.co.uk

www.gamblingcommission.gov.uk

www.gamingintelligence.com

www.independent.co.uk

www.metro.co.uk

www.ourculturemag.com

www.parentzone.org.uk

www.rsph.org.uk

www.schoolsweek.co.uk

www.telegraph.co.uk

www.theconversation.com

www.thecritic.co.uk

www.theguardian.com

www.uktechnews.co.uk

www.ukri.org

www.yougov.co.uk